Foreword

Britain reshaped the world not by building a great empire, but by opening up the continents through the steam railway. Invented by Cornish mining engineer Richard Trevithick, it appeared with a whimper rather than a bang, and it was left to others to develop and hone to as near perfection as possible.

Yet Britain did not invent the railway. The concept of using rails to guide trucks on wheels had been around for more than two millennia.

It is conjectured that railways and drama had a common beginning, back in ancient Greece, when some enterprising producer discovered that it was easy to move large sections of scenery if it was built on trolleys that ran on grooves carved into the stage floor.

In that halcyon age of drama and philosophy, the great Greek thinker Plato came up with his theory of forms. Somewhere up in the heavens, there is an ideal form of every object that manifests itself on earth.

For instance, in Plato's celestial consciousness there is the perfect table: we cannot see it or know exactly what it looks like, but can merely guess, and so the concept 'table' is produced in an infinite series of shapes, styles and sizes.

The same theory may be applied to every other object on the plant – including the railway.

When someone mentions railway engines, what is the first image that comes to mind? The world's most famous locomotive, *Flying Scotsman*, resplendent in LNER apple green? A streamlined A4 Pacific like *Mallard*, which holds the world railway steam speed record? A Great Western Railway 4-6-0 like *Lode Star* in the painting? A little blue tank engine with a plastic face and No 1 on its side? Or maybe just a bog standard black steam locomotive, either with a tender or side tanks, laden with coal and emitting large clouds of black smoke.

Others more in tune with the 'modern' railway than its heritage past the might immediately think of a Class 125 High Speed Train, a Eurostar unit or a suburban diesel multiple unit.

The fact is – as with Plato's table, there is no definitive or ideal version of exactly what a railway locomotive, or indeed a railway, should look like.

Like the table, the railway principle has manifested itself in a multitude of forms, each offering advantages and disadvantages over another, and several certainly verging on the bizarre or extreme by 'normal' perfections.

This volume is like no other railway book that you will have read before. It is an attempt to bring together Britain's most unusual railways in one volume – the radical, the different, the bold, the unorthodox, the experimental, the futuristic, the hidden lines, the bridges too far.

The railway principle is, of course, not just about the country's national network of main and branch lines. Individual industrial lines will produce bespoke systems, some with their own type of locomotives, often very unusual in appearance. In the steam age, there were thousands of industrial sidings and systems, many with a distinct character of their own.

Then we have cliff or funicular railways, in which the principle is used to ascend very steep gradients in a very short distance. ➤

The Romney Hythe & Dymchurch Railway is the world's smallest public double-track line. Davey Paxman 4-6-2 No 1 Green Goddess is seen heading towards *Dungeness*, a village largely comprising homes made from old wooden-bodied railway carriages. ROBIN JONES

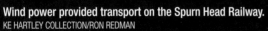

Wind power provided transport on the Spurn Head Railway. KE HARTLEY COLLECTION/RON REDMAN

This traction engine-like Aveling & Porter locomotive worked on Buckinghamshire's eccentric Wotton Tramway, which ended its days as part of the London Underground system! LONDON TRANSPORT

Author:
Robin Jones

Design:
Kelvin Clements, Leanne Cropley,
Justin Blackamore, Tim Pipes,
Charlotte Pearson
Production editor:
Janet Richardson
Advertising:
Carol Woods

Production manager:
Craig Lamb
Publisher:
Dan Savage
Commercial director:
Nigel Hole
**Business development
director:**
Terry Clark
Managing director:
Brian Hill

Published by:
Mortons Media Group Ltd,
Media Centre, Morton Way,
Horncastle, Lincs LN9 6JR
Tel: 01507 523456

Printed by:
William Gibbons & Son,
Wolverhampton
ISBN:
978-1-906167-25-7

www.mortonsbooks.co.uk

Britain's RTV31 hovertrain is preserved at Peterborough's Railworld museum along with a section of its test track. ROBIN JONES

Leaves on the line – or just sea kale on the shingle? This is one of the fish railways of Dungeness. ROBIN JONES

Cut-down Port of Par Bagnall saddle tanks *Judy* and *Alfred* reprising their Thomas the Tank Engine roles as Bill and Ben at the West Somerset Railway on 5 July 2009. This unique pair are now operating together for the first time in preservation. ERIC BROOM

They differ greatly from the idea of a 'normal' railway, but are so commonplace around the coast that they cannot as a group be considered to be 'weird'. However, take a look at the four-track underground Clifton Rocks Railway – every bit as fascinating as Brunel's Clifton Suspension Bridge above ground!

In this book I have tried to collect together the bizarre, the weird and wonderful, the out of-place, much of which can be seen today. What may have been run of the mill 70 years ago, such as cut-down steam locomotives, may be unique and eyecatching today.

We will begin by looking at Isambard Brunel and his 7ft 0¼in broad gauge, in so many ways superior to standard gauge, yet disappeared into the black hole of history.

There are the wonderful double-ended Fairlies articulated locomotives we can ride behind on the Ffestiniog Railway today.

Nearby runs the Snowdon Mountain Railway, Britain's only rack-and-pinion line, despite the fact that we invented the system!

Romney Marsh is so much more than the world's only double track mainly public railway in miniature, with its basic but ingenious fish railways across the Dungeness shingle and the nearby sprawling village made from old wooden-bodied carriages, several of which are now designer weekend retreats.

The sight of St Michael's Mount on the last leg of the train journey from London to Penzance has always had the 'wow' factor for passengers, but how many realise that a working railway runs right through the middle of this fairytale island, out of sight of the hundreds of thousands of visitors it receives each year.

Another island in the West Country, Steep Holm, appears to be little more than a lump of limestone when viewed from the mainland but not only had its own railway but a network – and it is still there, because it was too difficult for the scrapmen to rip up!

We also look at the private Statfold Barn Railway, where a myriad of traction from a rail-mounted Land Rover to an air pressure-powered steam locomotive have appeared in recent years, while the Hunslet Engine Company turns out brand new full-size steam locomotives from an adjacent workshop.

Who needs steam, when you can have electric power? Britain's first electric line was the Volk's Electric Railway in Brighton, while the world's first electric overhead line was the Liverpool Overhead Railway, again taking the railway concept into a new dimension. There again, can electric power be truly clean when it needs power station to generate it – the Spurn Head Railway may have had the answer with its two sail-powered vehicles!

And why bother with two rails when one is sufficient? We look at the legendary Listoswel & Ballybunion Railway in Ireland, and Britain's only steam monorail locomotive in Blaenau Ffestiniog.

There are those who thought that rails should be consigned to history, like the magnetic levitation train which once ran at Birmingham International Airport, or Britain's only hovertrain which topped 100mph in Cambridgeshire as the Government was pulling the plug on the project.

Indeed, the government of the day had a far deeper interest in railways than anyone imagined: below Corsham in Wiltshire, a railway system served an underground city which would have become the seat of power, housing the Royal Family, the Prime Minister and cabinet and the top brass in the event of a nuclear war. The conspiracy theorists were ridiculed when they argued for years it was there: in this volume, we have the pictures to prove it!

We round off our journey into the fascinating art of the railway possible with a TV stunt to rebuild 10 miles of the national network in just a week – using OO scale model track to relink Barnstaple with Bideford. How much more bizarre can you get? ∎

Robin Jones

Britain's WEIRDEST RAILWAYS
Contents

Two heads are better than one – at least on the Ffestiniog Railway, famous for its distinctive articulated double Fairlie locomotives. David Lloyd George, built at the railway's Boston Lodge Works in 1992, heads through slate country towards Blaenau Ffestiniog. FR

Big man, big locomotives, biggest gauge

Isambard Kingdom Brunel, voted the second greatest Briton of all time after Sir Winston Churchill in a TV poll, never hesitated to tear up the rule book in search of transport engineering excellence. His Great Western Railway was built to the massive 7ft ¼in broad gauge to link London to Wales, the West Country and the West Midlands – but despite its many clear advantages, the rest of the country did not follow suit. The system was finally scrapped in 1892, and very little survived for posterity. However, two of the massive world-beating express passenger engine types have been recreated in the heritage era – but only to run on very short demonstration lines.

In 1833, Nicholas Roch, a member of the Bristol Docks Committee, was asked to find an engineer to build a railway from the city to London.

The idea had been mooted before, but Bristol merchants had since become increasingly worried about safeguarding the position of Bristol as the second port in the country and the chief one for American trade in the face of growing competition from Liverpool, which was developing its own rail connection with the capital. The year before, four Bristol businessmen, John and William Harford, Thomas Guppy and George Jones, had resolved to act.

Roch approached his young friend

Isambard Kingdom Brunel, the great engineer to be, whose work on the city harbour and whose plans for a suspension bridge across the Avon Gorge at Clifton had won a competition in 1831.

Brunel told the scheme's backers that he would only survey a route that would be the best, not the cheapest – and after being told to survey the route within a month, Brunel set out on horseback and drew up his blueprint for what became the Great Western Railway. The enabling Parliamentary bill received Royal Assent on 31 August 1835 and construction began within a month, with Brunel appointed its engineer at the age of 27.

At the time, there was no national railway network as such. Designers and architects were left very much to 'do their own thing', and the net result was that one railway in one part of the country might well turn out to be very different to another.

Indeed, despite the steam locomotive having its first public demonstration in 1804, it was not until the Rainhill Trials of 1829, won by Stephenson's *Rocket*, that it was almost universally accepted as the way forward. Before it held the trials, the Liverpool & Manchester Railway had seriously considered using cable haulage rather than locomotives to pull its trains, and *Cycloped*, a contraption powered by a

North Star, the GWR's first locomotive, reassembled following its destruction at Swindon a century ago and now displayed in the town's STEAM museum. ROBIN JONES

Two new main line express passenger steam locomotives have been unveiled in Britain in the 21st century and on 29 August 2009 they were lined up at Didcot Railway Centre for the first time. Peppercorn A1 4-6-2 No 60163 *Tornado*, which has taken the national network by storm, attracting huge crowds wherever it goes since it was officially launched on the main line in January, is seen alongside replica broad gauge 2-2-2 *Fire Fly*, representing state-of-the-art steam traction of the 1840s, but which can travel only a few hundred yards on demonstration lines because there are no 7ft 0¼in routes left. Ironically, the last GWR broad gauge locomotive to be built was called *Tornado*. FRANK DUMBLETON/GREAT WESTERN SOCIETY

horse treading a drive belt on a truck, was entered into the competition.

This book deals with Britain's more unusual manifestations of the railway concept, but even in the decade that followed the trials, the notion of what constituted the 'normal' or 'ideal' railway was still very much in the melting pot.

Track gauge, the distance between rails, was one of the biggest issues of those formative years. Rocket designer George Stephenson came up with the rather odd figure of 4ft 8½in. Why not a round 4ft 6in or 5ft, you might well ask.

Stephenson's measurement was said to derive from calculations of the average space between the wheels of horse-drawn road carts in the North East, for early thinking was that such carts could be adapted to run on colliery railways. Whatever his reasons, his gauge caught on big time, and most new major railways in Britain, and later North America and the continent adopted it.

There was no legal obligation, however, for all railways to adopt the same gauge.

For instance, the Eastern Counties Railway built its first line, from London to Colchester, to 5ft gauge, but soon regretted the decision when directors realised that its trains could not run on and off the network of 4ft 8½in gauge lines that was rapidly covering Britain.

Opened on 28 March 1843, when the Eastern Counties' 5ft gauge line met what later became known as standard gauge, passengers and freight had to be taken off one train and transferred to another, creating delays and pushing up costs. So the Eastern Counties was converted to standard gauge during September and October 1844.

When the London & Blackwall Railway was built, opening in 1840/1 between Blackwall and Fenchurch Street, not only was it built to 5ft 0½in gauge, but its trains, both passenger and freight, were cable hauled. Its engineer: none other than George Stephenson's son Robert – who obviously did not have standardisation of gauges as the top of his priority list despite his father's preference for 4ft 8½in.

It did not employ state-of-the-art technology: the ropes continually broke, and the wire cables which superseded them in 1841 fared little better. When it was realised that other railway companies wanted to run over the route, cable haulage was finally scrapped and the line regauged to 4ft 8½in.

While George Stephenson came up with a gauge apparently based on historical practice, Brunel – a man who was to be internationally renowned for pushing technology and design to its utmost limits – insisting on starting with a blank sheet of paper, and choosing a brand new size

dictated purely by technology and logic. He wanted his railway built to a 7ft 0¼in gauge – the quarter inch being in there to accommodate clearances.

The omission of a clause stipulating the gauge from the GWR's Parliamentary Bill allowed Brunel to choose his own gauge. His choice was both radical and highly controversial, but he justified it on scientific grounds: indeed, it is still the broadest gauge to have been used for an extensive public passenger system. He explained to the GWR directors that 7ft 0¼in offered distinct advantages in reducing the centre of gravity of rolling stock by mounting coach and wagon bodies between the wheels rather than above them.

Furthermore, the much-wider gauge would offer bigger and more powerful locomotives and carriages and wagons with a greater capacity.

However, he acknowledged from the outset that it would be impossible for GWR trains to run over other lines built to 4ft 8½in gauge, admitting the tragic flaw that would bring down broad gauge.

Brunel did not want to compromise with everyone else. He wanted only the best – and there are many who believe today that had the world opted for his broad gauge, railways would have retained a far more important role in our modern world in ➤

The last broad gauge train to the west in Sonning Cutting, 20 May 1892. as painted by F Moore. NATIONAL RAILWAY MUSEUM

which they have long since been relegated to second place by motor transport.

In terms of technological development rarely does competition lead to standardisation, at least in the first instance. For instance, only in 2009 it has been announced that the makers of mobile telephones will band together to produce a standard socket for power chargers and other cables – the nuisance value and inconvenience of manufacturers having their own fittings is immeasurable.

Likewise, I have used Pentax single lens reflex cameras for nearly three decades, because my extensive collection of K fit

lenses will not fit on Canon or Nikon models and I cannot afford to buy a complete new set to fit a different camera mount. But would it not be great if there was a universal fitting?

The Stephensons may not have liked Brunel's choice of gauge, but Robert was more than happy to build him his first locomotive at Newcastle-upon-Tyne. The 2-2-2 *North Star*, originally built for the 5ft 6in gauge New Orleans Railway but regauged for Brunel, hauled the inaugural passenger train over the first section of 24 miles from Paddington to Maidenhead on 4 June 1838.

It was not until June 1841 that the GWR line from Bristol to London, a distance of 118 miles and in part nicknamed 'Brunel's billiard table' because of its smoothness, was completed throughout at a cost of £6,500,000, more than twice the original estimate, with breathtaking features such as Sonning Cutting, the gravity-defying elliptical-arched bridge at Maidenhead and the stupendous feat of early Victorian engineering that is Box Tunnel.

Some of Brunel's own early designs for broad gauge locomotives did not pass muster, but it was his appointment of 21-year-old Daniel Gooch as locomotive superintendent which won the day for him big time. Gooch set about designing a more powerful and larger version of the Star class, the Firefly class of 2-2-2s.

Seven manufacturers were contracted to build the 62 engines in the class, and the first was delivered by Jones, Turner & Evans of Newton-le-Willows on 12 March 1840. It was named *Fire Fly*, and a new era in British transportation was about to begin.

Fire Fly was chosen to pull the directors' special to mark the opening of the line beyond Twyford to Reading. The down run from Paddington took just 45mins for the 36 miles, while on the return an astonishing 58mph was reached and the 31 miles from Twyford to the capital completed in a mere 37mins.

Such high-speed running was unheard of in Britain or indeed any other country, and the Fire Fly class immediately showed it had the potential to achieve the four targets it had been set: speed, safety, reliability, and ease of maintenance.

Mixed gauge trackwork on the Didcot demonstration running line leading to the relocated Burlescombe transhipment shed. ROBIN JONES

Brunel and Gooch established Swindon Works where the GWR began building their own locomotives to the latter's specifications, and the move led to a succession of handsome, stable and powerful engines culminating in the superb Iron Duke class.

By the standards of the day, Gooch's locomotives recorded astonishing speeds and amazing start-to-stop times. The timings of the fastest Paddington-Didcot trains in 1848 were not bettered until the arrival of the Class 125 High Speed Train units nearly 130 years later.

Brunel also engineered the Bristol & Exeter Railway, effectively extending the GWR. On 1 May 1844, Fire Fly class locomotive *Actaeon* driven by Gooch covered the 194 miles from Paddington in an at-the-time unbelievable five hours. The return journey was even more spectacular, with Paddington reached in 4hrs 40mins, achieving a world-record average of 40.1mph for the two journeys.

On the same Wellington bank where *City of Truro* was to allegedly break the 100mph barrier in 1904, a Bristol & Exeter Railway broad gauge 4-2-4 tank engine reached 81.8mph.

So why did the rest of the country not take a leaf out of Brunel's book and converted the 7ft 0¼in gauge?

Standardisation is notorious for slowing down or even denying technological advancement. Anyone remember V2000 video recorders? Back in the early 1980s, the format was streets ahead of anything that Betamax or VHS could offer in terms of features on video players. Also, Betamax users claimed that their format was better than the bigger bulky VHS cartridges.

Yet VHS won the day by a mile, not necessarily on technological merit, but because it 'got in first', took the lion's share of the market and slowly but surely pushed the others out by offering a far wider range of products.

Parliament recommended banning broad gauge as early as 1845 in the interests of uniformity and to avoid breaks of gauges, with passengers having to change trains and freight unloaded and loaded again, even though it conceded that 7ft 0¼in was superior in terms of speed and safety. At that time there were 274 miles of broad gauge track compared to 1901 miles of 4ft 8½in gauge lines.

Despite Brunel's stubbornness over the gauge issue, a chink in his armour appeared in 1847 when the GWR began laying mixed gauge, between Gloucester and Cheltenham, in order to handle through trains.

The broad gauge empire expanded through South Wales to Milford Haven, Penzance in the far west, north to Wolverhampton and south to Weymouth. Some lines which never became part of the GWR empire, like Exeter to Barnstaple (London & South Western Railway) and the Somerset Central Railway (Burnham-on-Sea to Wells) even adopted 7ft 0¼in.

By 1866 broad gauge extended to 1427 miles, including around 387 miles of mixed gauge. However, it was still very much a London to the West Country, West Midlands and South Wales phenomenon.

The GWR built its first standard gauge engines in 1855, a year after absorbing its first 4ft 8½in gauge lines, the Shrewsbury & Chester and Shrewsbury & Birmingham railways.

Brunel died in 1859 and 10 years later, realising that the end for broad gauge was inevitable, the GWR authorised the conversion of the routes to Oxford, Birmingham and Wolverhampton to standard gauge, followed by the South Wales main line in May 1872.

However, some lines were still built to 7ft 0¼in gauge, the last being the St Ives branch which opened on 1 June 1877. Also, the Bristol & Exeter opened its broad gauge Cheddar Valley line from Yatton to Wells in 1869, converting it to standard gauge six years later.

The last GWR broad gauge engine outshopped from Swindon, Rover class 4-2-2 No 24 *Tornado*, emerged in July 1888. It ran for less than four years in traffic.

In 1891 the GWR board agreed to ditch broad gauge altogether, with only 171 route miles of pure broad gauge remaining. ➤

A typical GWR broad gauge signal, recreated at Didcot. ROBIN JONES

If you discount the reassembled non-working *North Star*, the sole surviving original main line company broad gauge locomotive is the South Devon Railway's 0-4-0VBT No 151 *Tiny*, which was also the smallest. SOUTH DEVON RAILWAY

When the last broad gauge lines were converted to 4ft 8½in by an army of 4200 workers during 21/22 May 1892, a total of 196 engines, 347 coaches and 3544 wagons remained. Around 15 miles of sidings were laid on a three-acre site at Swindon bought by the GWR specially to store them while they waited to be scrapped – as there was nowhere else where they could be used. (By comparison, you can still find Betamax recorders at car boot sales!).

On Friday 20 May, the last-ever broad gauge train left Penzance for Swindon at 9.57pm – 47mins late, due to the crowds who wanted to witness the system's last rites. The train stopped at literally every station between Penzance and Exeter, and on its

departure each stationmaster had to confirm to the inspector on board that all broad gauge stock had been removed from his station.

Only then, on receipt of each stationmaster's message, were the permanent way gangs allowed to rip up the broad gauge track behind the train and replace it with standard gauge.

The final GWR broad gauge engines to run were South Devon Railway 4-4-0STs *Leopard* and *Stag*, used until June 1893 at Swindon for shunting stock into the cutting shop at Swindon for scrapping.

Several broad gauge locomotives were offered in the 1890s to museums for display – without any track on which to run, they were good for nothing else – but in each

case the offer was declined, to the eternal regret of subsequent generations. Two were preserved by the GWR, *North Star* and *Lord Of The Isles*, but they were cut up at Swindon Works in 1906 to create storage space under the orders of none other than William Stanier, who made no secret about the fact that he was concerned about the future, not the past, and went on to design the great Pacific locomotives for the London, Midland & Scottish Railway.

However, enough parts were salvaged from this wanton act of vandalism for *North Star* to be reassembled as a stationary exhibit in 1925, and it is now displayed in STEAM – Museum of the Great Western Railway, at Swindon.

The sole surviving original main line company broad gauge locomotive is the South Devon Railway's 0-4-0 vertical-boilered tank engine No 151 *Tiny*, which was also the smallest. Bought to replace horses on Plymouth's Sutton harbour branch, it was withdrawn in 1883 and sent for use as a stationary boiler at Newton Abbot works, where it was restored and exhibited on the Down platform from 1927. It is now on static display in the modern-day South Devon Railway's Buckfastleigh museum, but cannot be said to be anywhere near representative of Brunel's 7ft 0¼in gauge system than Del Boy's Reliant Robin could claim to be typical of a motor industry which includes Rolls Royces, Aston Martins and Daimlers.

So GWR broad gauge with its larger-than-life locomotives with gleaming copper fireboxes, enormous driving wheels and stovepipe chimneys passed into history leaving only scant traces of its existence.

An *Illustrated London News* sketch of one of the first broad gauge trains over Brunel's stupendous Royal Albert Bridge at Saltash in Cornwall following its official opening by Prince Albert on 2 May 1859. BRUNEL 200

The replica of *Iron Duke* inside the Great Hall at the National Railway Museum. The importance of replicas like these cannot be overstated, for they represent a huge slice of world-beating British transport history that was all but wiped off the face of the earth in one weekend in 1892 and lost to future generations. ROBIN JONES

Its inclusion in this book poses one big question – while by today's perception Brunel's broad gauge can certainly be described as 'unusual' because of its by-comparison outsize proportions, was it the rest of the national railway network that warrants the label 'weird' for not adopting it despite its many contemporary advantages?

On a very small scale, some 7ft 0¼in gauge lines remained in use into the 20th century, at isolated outposts such as the Holyhead breakwater railway, and on a harbour line in the Azores. Incidentally, even broader gauges were to be found in Britain: the Dalzell Iron & Steel Works in Motherwell bought three new 10ft 11in gauge Barclay 0-4-0STs to haul ladles of molten slag on an internal line.

The clear advantages of the 7ft 0¼in gauge system were not forgotten; in 1928, engineer W Collard published plans for a Brunel broad gauge railway from London to Paris via a Channel Tunnel. Hitler dreamed of going one better, and formulated plans for a three-metre (9ft 9ins) gauge trans-European super railway capable of carrying ships on bogie wagons.

Broad gauge steam has since staged a heritage era comeback.

The National Railway Museum at York had a replica Iron Duke class 4-2-2 built for the Great Western 150 celebrations in 1985, using parts from two standard gauge industrial Austerity 0-6-0 saddle tanks including a boiler, and a demonstration running line was laid outside. The new Iron Duke became the first broad gauge engine to steam in Britain since 1893, and had a replica

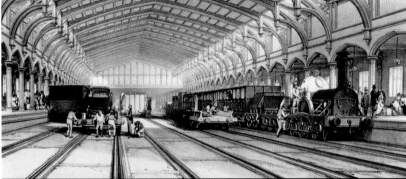

A JC Bourne sketch of the interior of Brunel's original Temple Meads terminus at Bristol, with a broad gauge train standing in one of the platforms. BRUNEL 200A JC Bourne sketch of the interior of Brunel's original Temple Meads terminus at Bristol, with a broad gauge train standing in one of the platforms. BRUNEL 200

carriage made to go with it. It is now on static display inside the museum's Great Hall.

Didcot Railway Centre, home of the Great Western Society, also has a 7ft 0¼in gauge running line, leading to the former Burlescombe transhipment shed, where in the days of the break of gauge, passengers and goods were switched from one train to another. On it runs an all-new replica of *Fire Fly*.

Aided by the rediscovered original drawings by Daniel Gooch for the Firefly class at Paddington, retired Royal Navy Commander John Mosse founded the Firefly Trust in 1982 to build a replica. By 1987, sufficient money had been raised to allow building to start, as a Manpower Services Community project backed by Bristol City Council. When funding was

withdrawn, the project found a new home at Didcot, where *Fire Fly* ran under its own power for the first time at Didcot on 2 March 2005. It was the first new main line steam locomotive to be built in Britain since BR standard 9F 2-10-0 *Evening Star* 45 years before.

Yet where can the modern Iron Duke or *Fire Fly* run apart from demonstration lines? Could a new broad gauge heritage railway be built to carry fare-paying passengers, to replicate the great days of speed on the Bristol & Exeter and recapture lost glories?

There again, 7ft 0¼in gauge is still in commercial use at one location in Britain today. An electric crane runs along a 151ft-long track at the National Rivers Authority depot in Reading, a stop on Brunel's original GWR main line. ∎

A truly atmospheric railway: the pumping station at Dawlish in a painting by Condy, with the vacuum pipe running between the rails. ELTON COLLECTION, IRONBRIDGE GORGE MUSEUM TRUST

A truly atmospheric railway

Beautiful, brilliant, but foolish? Isambard Kingdom Brunel jumped years ahead of steam locomotive haulage when he opened his South Devon Atmospheric Railway – but was let down by the available technology of his day. Furthermore, his famous seaside main line route through Dawlish and Teignmouth is now the most expensive stretch of the national network to maintain, because he insisted on building it at the foot of cliffs just a few feet above the waves.

In September 1844, Isambard and Daniel Gooch joined other eminent engineers of the day to witness a demonstration by inventors Samuel Clegg and Jacob Samuda of an atmospheric train on Ireland's one-and-a-half-mile-long Dalkey & Kingstown Railway.

Clegg, a gas lighting pioneer, and Samuda, a marine engineering expert, had patented an atmospheric system of propulsion on 3 January 1838.

Their method consisted of a cast-iron tube laid between rails and sealed by airtight valves at each end. A piston linked to the bottom of a carriage was pushed past the valve into the tube, and huge stationary steam engines located on the side of the railway pumped air out of the tube, generating a vacuum ahead of the piston.

The greater pressure of the atmosphere behind the piston would force it along the tube and pull the carriage with it, without the need for a locomotive.

Brunel and his father Marc had over a decade before looked in vain at pressured carbonic gas-powered alternatives to the steam locomotive, foreseeing the day when it would

become obsolete. However, when he saw atmospheric propulsion at work, he believed he had stumbled on the new way ahead.

One of the biggest complaints about steam trains in the days of roofless carriages was that they showered passengers with hot water and cinders. Yet Clegg and Samuda offered a system which was clean, silent and fast.

Furthermore, since there was no engine, the trains would be lighter and more efficient, and building a railway would accordingly be less expensive.

Steep gradients could be tackled without having to bring in an additional locomotive to add extra power. Indeed, the atmospheric system presented all the advantages of the electric traction that we enjoy today.

Prime Minister Sir Robert Peel was so impressed by the atmospheric system that he wanted to see all railways adopt it.

After the Dublin & Kingstown Railway came the London & Croydon in 1846, and the 1.4-mile Paris & St-Germain Railway from Bois de Vezinet to St-Germain in Paris in 1847. They were followed by Brunel's South Devon Railway.

Three of the total of nine atmospheric railway pumping stations survive today, but only the one at Starcross (below) was ever used. The Totnes example, part of a derelict dairy, was saved from demolition in 2008 when English Heritage listed it following a massive local outcry, and another still stands at Torre. ROBIN JONES

After completing the Bristol & Exeter Railway in 1836, Isambard planned to create a 7ft 0¼in gauge route all the way from Paddington to Penzance. However, his early surveys for a main line from Exeter to Plymouth highlighted many gradients over which the steam trains of the day might well struggle.

His preferred route ran over Dartmoor foothills to the west of Newton Abbot like Hemerdon, Dainton and Rattery, all of which were later to become legendary in terms of proving locomotive and crew performances.

Yet because atmospheric traction did not rely on the adhesion of heavy locomotives to the rails, he could economise on earthworks and allow such steep inclines. To boost power on the heavy gradients, with atmospheric propulsion all you had to do would be to increase the vacuum pipe diameter, add a second pipe, or build a bigger pumping station.

Appointed as engineer to the South Devon Railway which received its Royal Assent on 4 July 1844, he convinced its directors that huge savings would be made by using Clegg and Samuda's system over the entire 52-mile route – despite misgivings both from his acclaimed locomotive superintendent Daniel Gooch and Robert Stephenson.

In line with Brunel's blending of classical styles of architecture with cutting-edge

transport technology, seven huge Italianate engine houses were built at three-mile intervals along the route from Exeter to Newton Abbot – which followed the coast and created a stunningly picturesque route through a series of tunnels linking romantic red-sand beaches and coves.

The construction of this stretch of the route may be viewed either as an engineering marvel of the day, or as an absurdity. It hugged the foot of storm-lashed cliffs and cliffs and nowadays is the most expensive part of Britain's national

rail network to maintain due to marine erosion and rock falls, with regular stoppages and delays.

The South Devon atmospheric system struggled from the outset, probably because it was built before its principles had been sufficiently tested. It was quickly realised that the planned 12in vacuum pipe needed to be replaced by one of 15in diameter, and so the pumping engines already installed along the route had to run faster than their design speed in order to maintain the vacuum. ➤

This first section of the South Devon Railway opened on 30 May 1846 – using steam engines at first, while the vacuum tube and leather and metal valve of the atmospheric system continued to be laid.

Two public atmospheric trains ran over the line from 13 September 1847, and from 10 January 1848 services were extended to Newton Abbot, with some freight being carried. The high speeds promised by Brunel were indeed achieved– 68mph with a 28-ton load and 35mph with 100 tons, but the 20-mile journey from Exeter to Newton Abbot with four stops took a slow 55 minutes due to one train having to wait for the other to pass as it was the route was still single track.

Brunel may have been ahead of his time, but supporting technologies were not up there with him. The hinge of the airtight valve and the ring around the piston were both made of leather, an organic material which was totally unsuitable for the purpose, as had just been proved to be the case on the Croydon line, which scrapped its atmospheric system that year after repeated breakdowns.

Brunel's answer was to employ a large team of men to continually apply a sticky sealant on the valve to make it airtight. The sealant then proved useless after exposure to the air, so a new compound using cod-liver oil and soap was tried without much better success. This compound, along with natural oils in the leather, was sucked into the vacuum pipe, and the leather dried and cracked in the sun, wind and salty air. It was also gnawed by rats.

Air leaked into the pipe through the cracks in the leather and so the steam pumps had to work much harder and burn more coal to keep up the pressure.

However, there was no other suitable flexible material available in the mid-1800s. Two miles of the valve had to be completely replaced, while it was found that the vacuum pipes had been cast too roughly, and also the stationary steam engine pumps kept breaking down.

Brunel also failed to extend the line's electric telegraph system to the pumping stations. Had this been done, much costly and wasteful pumping would have been avoided.

Once teething problems had been overcome, the atmospheric railway performed well, with nine trains a day operating between Exeter and Teignmouth during spring and summer 1848, reaching average speeds of 64mph. They were well liked by passengers – apart from those travelling third class who were asked to get out and push when they broke down.

However, it was found that it cost 37 pence per mile to run an atmospheric train compared to 16 pence for steam.

Alarmed by soaring losses and vast amounts of unexpected expenditure, the directors confronted the absent Brunel at

A surviving section of atmospheric railway vacuum pipe subsequently used for decades as a culvert on Goodrington Sands is now displayed at Didcot Railway Centre. ROBIN JONES

While no atmospheric railway carriage has survived, a 5in gauge working model of a South Devon Railway train was built in the early 21st century by Barometer World at Merton in North Devon, a firm whose business is based around the concept of air pressure! There is no driver but a guard to operate the brake: today's Dockland Light Railway has driverless trains. BAROMETER WORLD

his home in Duke Street in London to demand explanations. Brunel blamed Clegg and Samuda for the failings of their system, and said that the only solution was to replace the pipes and the steam pumps.

With the railway's shareholders having lost nearly £500,000, the directors voted to scrap the system and opt for steam locomotive haulage as from 10 September 1848.

While the whole route opened throughout on 2 April 1849, the atmospheric system had not penetrated further south than Newton Abbot, although a pumping station was build at Totnes and another at Torre for a proposed branch, neither being used.

The world's other three atmospheric railways were also converted to steam. As a steam line, the South Devon Railway proved hugely successful, and was eventually converted to double track throughout to accommodate increasing volumes of traffic. It became part of the Great Western Railway on 1 February 1876.

Yet what if the materials and research to make the atmospheric system work had been available? Could it have presented a serious competitor to steam haulage more than a century before the advent of diesel and electric locomotive on the British main line?

There still remains the problem of the sea wall route.

Preserved GWR 4-6-0s Nos 5051 *Earl Bathurst* and 4930 *Hagley Hall* storm through Horse Cove tunnel with a Bristol-Plymouth charter in July 1985 during the Great Western Railway 150 celebrations. They did not make it, breaking down on the South Devon banks despite doubling up! Brunel foresaw such problems with steam traction on the route a century before, and that is why he opted for the atmospheric system. BRIAN SHARPE

Some experts predict that global warming will see sea levels rise by at least 20in in the next half century, and some of the most modern diesel multiple units have found difficulty in running over the route after storms.

In 2002, engineers battled the tides to complete a £2.4-million project to strengthen the sea wall, with 12,000 cubic metres of concrete poured into trenches at its base to stop the sea undermining it, and over 500 steel bars inserted into the cliff for stability.

Serious plans to replace the route altogether were drawn up in the steam age itself.

In 1936, a £3-million scheme for an avoiding line about a mile inland running from Exminster to Bishopsteignton was mooted by the GWR, which bought parcels of land, cleared undergrowth and marked the route out, before the Second World War suspended proceedings forever.

From 1903 onwards, the GWR used the single-track Teign Valley line via Heathfield, Chudleigh and Ide as a diversionary route between Exeter and Newton Abbot during bad weather, but British Railways saw fit to close it in 1958.

Neither available any more is the Southern Railway's main line from Exeter to Plymouth via Okehampton, which beyond Coleford Junction is now the Dartmoor Railway heritage and freight line, and which ends at Meldon Quarry. Persistent calls have been made for the reinstatement of the missing section between Meldon, Tavistock and Bere Alston. A storm-free alternative route for long-distance non-stopping services is surely vital to safeguard the future of rail transport to the south-west peninsula.

And there remains the question, which was more bizarre: Brunel's experiment with atmospheric traction, or the coastal route on which it was laid? ■

Two of the GWR's 3501 class of broad gauge 2-4-0 tender locomotives haul a train over the sea wall route at Teignmouth. BROAD GAUGE SOCIETY

David Lloyd George, the world's newest double Fairlie, runs along the deviation above Llyn Ystradau reservoir, with the original route of the railway visible on the foreshore **below.** ROGER DIMMICK/FR

Merddin Emrys at Porthmadog Harbour station in May 2005. JAMES WAITE/FR

Double Fairlie *Merddin Emrys* runs through a sylvan stretch of the Ffestiniog Railway which it has served for 130 years. FR

The fabulous Fairlies!

One of the strangest yet most striking steam locomotive types of all to be seen in Britain today is the double Fairlie, immortalised by its association with the Ffestiniog Railway. Looking as if they are two ordinary engines joined back to back, the Victorian design proved so successful at negotiating tight curves that two examples have been built in modern times. Yet how much do they owe to a clandestine love affair that nearly landed their designer in jail?

In the 1840s, Newcastle-upon-Tyne engineer George England founded his own locomotive building company in New Cross, Surrey, It supplied one of the earliest tank engines to the contractors building the Newhaven branch of the London Brighton and South Coast Railway and exhibited another at The Great Exhibition in 1851.

The company went on to supply locomotives to several other railways, ranging from the Great Western and Caledonian down to the 1ft 11½in gauge Festiniog Railway in North Wales. There, between 1863-7, they delivered six 0-4-0 saddle tanks, four of which survive, two in working order.

The oldest surviving railway company in the world (its name was changed in the heritage era to include both fs in the name of the locality, an omission from the original act of Parliament which empowered it in 1832), the Festiniog was originally a horse-drawn affair, but in October 1863 steam locomotives were introduced, to allow longer slate trains to be run. This move also facilitated the official introduction of passenger trains in 1865, and it doing so it became first narrow-gauge railway in Britain to carry passengers.

England's long-time business associate was Robert Francis Fairlie, who was born either in 1830 or 1831 in Glasgow, and opting for railway engineering as a career, trained in the works at Crewe and Swindon before becoming locomotive

superintendent at the Londonderry & Coleraine Railway in 1852. Four years later he joined the Bombay, Baroda & Central India Railway before returning to London in 1859 where he set himself up as a railway engineering consultant.

In April 1862, England brought a criminal action against Fairlie in a case which modern observers might well consider bizarre.

At the Central Criminal Court, England alleged perjury on the part of Fairlie – who had eloped with his daughter Eliza Anne England. In order to obtain a marriage licence, Fairlie had sworn a false affidavit that her father had consented to the union, which he certainly had not done; after their wedding, the pair eloped to Spain. ➤

Earl of Merioneth running round the spiral loop above Dduallt Halt. ROGER DIMMICK/FR

The Festiniog Railway's first Fairlie, *Little Wonder*, at Porthmadog in the 1870s. FR CO ARCHIVES

If the case had been proved, Fairlie would most likely have been sent to prison. However, under cross-examination from Fairlie's representative, England admitted that he had run away with his present companion, Eliza's mother – and that he had a wife living at that time. He had lived with this lady several years but could not marry her until his wife died.

Under contemporary English law, a child born out of wedlock was considered nobody's child. Therefore in law she was nothing to do with England and could marry anyone without needing his permission.

So there no case to answer and therefore a verdict of not guilty was returned.

It is assumed that at the time there was great animosity between England and Fairlie. However, the rift healed sufficiently for England to build the first of a remarkable series of engines for the Festiniog Railway to a Fairlie patent of 1864.

Fairlie was convinced that the conventional pattern of locomotive was seriously deficient, because they wasted weight on unpowered wheels (and on a tender that did nothing but carry fuel and water without contributing to the locomotive's adhesive weight. Also, 'normal' locomotives had a quite different front and rear, and were not intended to be driven in reverse for long periods, thereby necessitating the provision of a turntable or turning triangle at every terminus.

To Fairlie, the obvious solution answer was have a double-ended locomotive, one which carried all its fuel and water aboard the locomotive and with every axle driven (the maximum tractive effort of any locomotive is limited by the power of its driving wheels).

His double-ended design was achieved by having two boilers on the locomotive, joined

Double Fairlie *Livingston Thompson* of 1885, now on static display in the National Railway Museum at York, is pictured at Tan-y-Bwlch in 1988. FR

back-to-back at the firebox ends, with the smokeboxes at each end, with controls at both ends of the central cab to allow the locomotive to be driven equally well in either directions.

The locomotive was supported on two swivelling powered bogies with all wheels driven. Steam was delivered from the boilers to the cylinders via flexible tubing. There were side tanks beside each boiler for the water supply, and bunkers for the fuel located above them.

Fairlie's first double-ended locomotive, *Pioneer*, was built by James Cross & Co of St Helens supplied to the standard gauge Neath & Brecon Railway in 1865, but it was not successful. Others went to the Queensland Railways in Australia, which were not happy with them and returned them to the builder.

However, *Little Wonder*, built by England in 1869 for the Festiniog, was a different

matter, and it brought its designer overnight fortune and fame.

On the Festiniog, which was built to carry slate from the pits of Blaenau Ffestiniog to the harbour at Porthmadog, Little Wonder was tested against the England saddle tanks, which themselves have been hailed as the first ever successful narrow gauge steam locomotive design.

George England retired in 1869, and Robert Fairlie joined with George England's son and JS Fraser to take over his works and to form the Fairlie Engine & Steam Carriage Co. George England junior died within a few months, and the works were sold, locomotive production ceasing at the end of 1870. The Fairlie Engine & Rolling Stock Co continued as an office for design and for the licensing of Fairlie locomotive manufacture.

Half a double Fairlie: single Fairlie *Taliesin* hauls the Ffestiniog Railway's vintage workmen's train. FR

'The rift healed sufficiently for England to build the first of a remarkable series of engines for the Festiniog Railway to a Fairlie patent of 1864.'

On 11 February 1870, Fairlie invited locomotive engineers from all over the world to the Festiniog Railway to see his invention. Railways as far afield at Russia, Mexico, Turkey and Sweden were represented. The event was a huge success, and left Fairlie with a bulging order book: not only that, but it did much to promote narrow gauge steam, demonstrating that it was a credible alternative to standard gauge in hill terrain. The Fairlie design meant that the fireboxes and ashpans were not restricted by frame or track width, but only by the overall loading gauge. By 1876, 43 different railways had operated his engines. However, the only railways where the type was truly successful in the long term was Mexico, New Zealand and the Festiniog. More than 50 Fairlies were supplied to Mexico over four decades, including 49 massive 0-6-0+0-6-0s which remained in use until the 1920s.

The problems many of the buyers found were the limited capacity for fuel and water caused by the lack of a tender, the flexible steam pipes being prone to leakage and wasting of power and the absence of unpowered wheels, which on 'normal' types of steam locomotive act as stabilisers. Early Fairlies had a tendency for rough riding and were more susceptible to derailments: *Little Wonder* was worn out and replaced by the Festiniog after less than two decades of intensive use. ➤

Standard gauge Fairlie locomotive Victoria with a typical Burry Port & Gwendreath Valley Railway holiday train believed to be at Pontyates. BRIAN CRIPPS COLLECTION

A late 50s scene at Harbour station, with *Livingston Thompson*, then named *Taliesin*, hauling a rake of stock in the green livery of the early heritage era.

Merddin Emrys heads below Rhiw Goch on 25 August 2009 ROGER DIMMICK/FR

Fairlie also produced 'single' versions, resembling 'normal' locomotives. Effectively a double Fairlie cut in half, they had a single articulated power bogie combined with an unpowered bogie under the cab, maintaining the ability to negotiate sharp turns. Popular in the USA, a single Fairlie 0-4-4 tank ran on the Swindon Marlborough & Andover Railway and three 0-6-4Ts were bought by the North Wales Narrow Gauge Railways, predecessor of the Welsh Highland Railway.

Fairlie gave the Festiniog Railway Company a perpetual licence to use the Fairlie locomotive patent without restriction in return for using the line to demonstrate Little Wonder – which became the first of six to be owned by the company.

George England died in 1878 and Fairlie followed on 31 July 1885.

The Ffestiniog is one of Europe's most spectacular heritage railways, weaving its way through Snowdonia's slate country, and one of its trademark features is the regular use of double Fairlies. Indeed, in modern times, it has made the type its own.

The second double Fairlie to arrive was *James Spooner*, which became the line's No 8. Supplied by Avonside, it lasted in service until 1933 when it was scrapped, the fate which befell *Little Wonder* in 1882.

The line's third double Fairlie, No 10 *Merddin Emrys*, named after the sixth century Welsh poet, was delivered in 1879 and is still in service today. It underwent a major rebuild in 1987/8 with new tanks.

No 11 *Livingston Thompson* was built at the line's own Boston Lodge works in 1886. Now

David Lloyd George at Rhiw Goch on 22 February 2003 IAN BUTTERS

out of service, it has been restored for static display, and is another star exhibit in the Great Hall at the National Railway Museum in York.

The Ffestiniog Railway had fallen derelict after World War Two, but following the success of the Talyllyn Railway revival led in 1951, the line was taken over by volunteers in 1954, under the leadership of businessman Alan Pegler, who in 1963 bought *Flying Scotsman* from British Railways. The revivalists began to reopen the railway in stages from Porthmadog Harbour station and finally reached Blaenau Ffestiniog on 25 May 1982, the 150th Anniversary of Royal Assent to the Festiniog Railway Act of 1832. In reopening the line, the revivalists had to create

a deviation around the Central Electricity Generating Board's Llyn Ystradau reservoir which had flooded part of the original line. The deviation included a spiral loop atypical of the Darjeeling Himalayan Railway but not Britain, and if only because the volunteers had to hack their way through the side of a mountain, must be considered one of the greatest achievements of the preservation era.

To cope with the extra demand for motive power as their line grew longer, the revivalists needed more motive power – and what better than to continue the Boston Lodge tradition by building their own?

In 1979, a new double Fairlie 0-4-4-0 with rather utilitarian modern box-like side tanks, *Earl of Merioneth* emerged from the works.

James Spooner became the Ffestiniog's second double Fairlie in 1872. FR CO ARCHIVES

The original Welsh Highland Railway was operated by the Ffestiniog Railway which provided some locomotives and stock. *James Spooner* is seen at South Snowdon in 1923/24. While this locomotive was scrapped, its rods and wheels are now part of *Livingston Thompson*.

It was so well received that a second, *David Lloyd George*, which has a more conventional appearance, emerged three years later.

The Ffestiniog has also owned a single Fairlie, the 1876-built *Taliesin*, which was scrapped in 1935. A replica was built at Boston Lodge in 1999 – using some parts from the original: there are those who would therefore like to consider it a 'rebuild' rather than a copy.

The railways Fairlies were designed to burn coal. Following trials in 1971, they were modified to burn oil. However, with the price of fuel soaring, *Earl of Merioneth* was converted to coal in 2005 having been built as an oil burner. *Merddin Emrys* was back-converted to coal burning in 2007.

Josephine, a double Fairlie, is preserved in New Zealand's South Island at Dunedin, and a 60cm gauge double Fairlie tramway type engine that ran on a French narrow gauge line is at the

Dresden Transport Museum in East Germany.

Until recently, it was thought that there were no other double Fairlies or remains thereof surviving in Britain.

However, in June 2004, Heritage Railway magazine revealed that two boilers from scrapped standard gauge double Fairlies had been rediscovered in Burry Port in South Wales. The discovery was made by the Gwendreath Railway Society, which wants to reopen the Burry Port & Gwendreath Valley Railway on which they ran.

It is believed that one of the boilers belonged to an 0-4-4-0T originally named *Pioneer* but later renamed *Mountaineer* and which in 1869 was only the second engine to be built by the Fairlie Steam & Carriage Company. The other boiler is believed to come from 0-6-6-0T *Victoria*, one of the abovementioned early Fairlies returned from Queensland, and later sold to the Burry Port

line. Scrapped around the turn of the century, the boilers are now 6ft underground – in use as stormwater culverts!

The society has made the local authority aware of its interest in the boilers, which are said to be in reasonable condition taking their use for the past century into account.

Undoubtedly they are historically valuable artefacts, and will be retrieved if ever the chance presents itself. While they could not be considered themselves as the basis for any new-build locomotive project, they could be used as a template to build a new boiler, or two. Who knows: one day, the Ffestiniog may lose its monopoly on double Fairlies in Wales!

Fairlie's invention may seem weird by comparison with other steam locomotives today, but he was not far wide of the mark. Most main line diesels and traction units today have cabs at either end and turntables are a comparative rarity on the national network. ■

The 'Brio' line that built London Bridge

Built to last: the uppermost part of the Haytor Granite Tramway is still very much intact. Haytor and its quarries are to the left.

The ultimate in 'green' transport – a railway made from natural materials on the spot, emitted no smoke or fumes, ran on straw and bags of oats and never rusted away despite 150 years of disuse. Welcome to the Dartmoor's unique Haytor Granite Tramway, which in 1820 was a last attempt at flying in the face of steam traction.

A Brio train set operates on much the same principles at the Haytor Tramway.

I have always loved Dartmoor, forever entranced by its dark and mysterious landscape at all seasons of the year. The many mysteries that it holds, its unique sense of foreboding yet at the same time welcoming atmosphere, and the feeling that there is always something new waiting round the corner to be discovered.

Among its greatest treasures is one of Britain's most curious railways of all.

Prized for its fine grain and high quality, Dartmoor granite has been a source of building material from neolithic times when it was used to build dwellings and the stone rows and circles which survive on the barren uplands today.

From the 1730s, ball clay, which is formed by decomposing granite, was mined in the Bovey Tracey area for use in pottery, and was carried away by pack mules for shipping from Newton Abbot via the Teign estuary.

James Templer, an orphan boy who made his fortune in India after running away to sea, bought the 80,000-acre Stover Estate near Newton Abbot on his return in 1865

at the age of 43. In 1781 he built a new mansion there using stone quarried from his quarries at Haytor, today one of the West Country's best-loved beauty spots.

He died in 1792, the year that his eldest son, also called James, influenced by the canal mania which facilitated the growth of the Industrial Revolution throughout Britain, opened a one-and-three-quarter-mile artificial waterway from Ventiford near the estate to Newton Abbot to improve transport for the movement of ball clay and also lignite and iron ore, which were also found in the locality.

It was the first artificial waterway to be built in Devon since the Exeter Ship Canal in the 16th century.

Five locks facilitated a rise of 19ft 3in over the short canal. Once opened, it brought much prosperity to the surrounding area, with 17 barges operating and ball clay being supplied to the great Thomas Wedgwood & Sons potteries at Stoke-on-Trent, and land prices tripled along its length.

George Templer, son of the second

James, developed the granite quarries at Haytor on a commercial basis, in response to demand for quality building materials.

However, if the quarries were to realise their true potential, a faster and more efficient mode of transport than horse-drawn carts over moorland tracks was needed.

George Templer came up with the idea of a railway. That in itself was by no means an original idea; the Tanfield Railway in County Durham boasts that it is the world's oldest line still in use, its ancestry dating back to 1725.

Steam traction had subsequently been invented by Richard Trevithick, his first public demonstration of a railway locomotive taking place in 1804, but had yet to take off in a big way: indeed, there were many who two decades later were still not convinced of its merits, and so Templer looked no further than the time-honoured use of horse traction.

However, George Templer's horse-worked railway would be very different to others that had gone before.

The Haytor quarries in their heyday of the 1820s.

A point and a siding.

One of the 'point' frogs on the tramway.

Tree on the line!

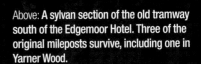

Above: A sylvan section of the old tramway south of the Edgemoor Hotel. Three of the original mileposts survive, including one in Yarner Wood.

Below: The only surviving bridge on the tramway crosses the Bovey Leat near Chapple Farm, about two miles west of Bovey Tracey.

Suitable iron for rails was not easily available in the region at the time – cast iron was brittle and had a habit of breaking on early railways – so his scheme involved the track being made from granite blocks, appropriately quarried at Haytor and cut to size, with a rebate carved in each for carrying the iron wheels of the wagons.

It was a 4ft 3in gauge plateway or flanged way, in which the guiding flanges that kept the wagons on the rails were part of the rails. The rails or 'tramplates' were carved from irregular blocks of solid granite laid directly on the ground.

The end result was not unlike a modern-day child's Brio wooden train set, which is based around blocks of track with grooves carved into them for the push-along trains to run on. Like Brio, Templer's system was capable of having all the usual features of trackwork – points, crossovers and sidings. At the points, the wheels were guided by wooden 'point tongues' made from oak, pivoted on the granite-block rails.

The granite rails had L-shaped grooves with the flanges on the inside. The iron

wheels of the wagons soon wore the straight granite flanges to shape on the curves.

The Haytor tramway was all but unique, the only other known example of this type of railway being a very short 3ft gauge limestone operation at Conisborough near Doncaster.

Going uphill, the empty wagons were hauled back to the quarries by teams of horses, but downwards, the loaded wagons moved by gravity to the Stover Canal basin at Ventiford,

The wooden flat-topped wagons had iron flangeless wheels and ran in trains of usually 12 vehicles drawn by around 18 horses in single file, in front for the upward journey and at the back for the downward trips.

The wagons were probably adapted road vehicles and were about 13ft long, with a 10ft wheelbase of 10ft (3.0m). The wheels were loose on the axles, and accidents were commonplace as the only braking was provided by the horses and long wooden poles forced against the wheels. Today's health and safety legislators would not be amused. ➤

An old sailor called Thomas Taverner was inspired by the tramway to write a poem:

Nineteen stout horses it was known,
From Holwell Quarry drew the stone,
And mounted on the twelve-wheeled car
'Twas safely brought from Holwell Tor

The '12-wheeled car' refers to 12 wagons with wheels'.

Taking a modern view, you might consider it to be a perfect 'green' form of transport with a minor carbon footprint. The stone blocks to make the track were quarried locally, and did not require iron to be smelted at polluting blast furnaces; there were no smoky emissions from steam engine chimneys and the form of traction was renewable – all you had to do was grow another field of hay or oats to keep it running.

The Haytor Granite Tramway, as it came to be known, may seem primitive when compared to its iron counterparts, but it has outlasted many of them including the northern end of the Moretonhampstead branch which superseded it. Indeed, when we talk about preserved or heritage railways, the Haytor Tramway may be considered a near-perfect example, because the rails do not rust, have no scrap value and are still in place along much of the route today.

However, in historical terms, we may also look at it as a 'last blast' from the age before steam traction was widely adopted as the only way ahead.

A complex of six branches and sidings akin to a marshalling yard sprang up around the busy Haytor quarries, and a line eight-and-a-half miles long descended from the 1300ft-high heather-clad moorland along a circuitous route into the Bovey valley, eventually reaching Ventiford basin at the northern end of the Stover Canal,

which had been extended westwards to Teigngrace meet it in 1820.

Built without an Act of Parliament, the tramway was officially opened on 16 September that year amid public celebrations and much rejoicing.

A contemporary account of the opening day ran as follows:

"On Saturday Mr Templer, of Stover House, gave a grand fete champetre on Haytor Down, on the completion of the granite rail road. The company assembled at its foot on Bovey Heathfield, and in procession passed over it to the rock. A long string of carriages, filled with elegant and beautiful females, multitudes of horsemen, the workmen on foot, the waggons covered with laurels and waving streamers, formed in their windings through the valley, an attractive scene to spectators on the adjacent hill. Old Haytor seemed alive: its sides were lined with groups of persons, and on its top a proud flag fluttered in the wind.

"Never," writes the ecstatic reporter of an Exeter paper, "was the Haytor's sod graced with such blooming fair ones, nor did it ever before display so festive a scene."

From Teigngrace the granite was carried by canal boat to the New Quay at Teignmouth for export by ship, the quay having been built in 1827 for the purpose.

The following decade saw several thousands of tons of granite shipped via the tramway each year.

In 1825, it carried granite for the building of no less a structure than

London Bridge, the one which in the 1960s was sold to the Americans. Indeed, it has been mooted that Templer's contract for supplying materials for the bridge was the prime reason for building the tramway in the first place.

Part of the British Museum, the old General Post Office in London and the Waltham Monument in Ludgate Circus were built from Haytor granite in the 19th century. The last use of Haytor granite was the building of the Exeter War Memorial.

Templer's personal spending greatly diminished his prosperity and in January 1829 he sold the Stover Estate along with the tramway and canal, to Edward Adolphus Seymour, the 11th Duke of Somerset.

Templer left Devon, returning a few years later when he built a new mansion at Sandford Orleigh on the outskirts of Newton Abbot. He became the granite company's chief agent in the county.

A proposal to mine iron ore as well as granite from

The New Quay at Teignmouth in 1827 with a large crane and blocks of cut granite ready for transhipment.

HAYTOR

Section later used as Moretonhampstead Branch

Stover Canal Basin

The level crossing is maintained, but the rest of the line is buried beneath undergrowth. This is the surviving part of the Moretonhampstead branch, still nominally part of the national rail network!

Haytor and ship it via the tramway came to nothing, and a decline in quarrying set in.

Templer was killed in a hunting accident in 1843, and despite a resurgence in demand for Haytor stone in the early 1850s, with the quarries employing around 100 men, trade had all but died out by 1858 in the face of competition from cheaper Cornish granite. By then, the Haytor Tramway had long since fallen into disuse.

Isambard Kingdom Brunel's broad gauge South Devon Railway opened to Newton Abbot on 30 December 1846 and was extended to Plymouth by 2 April 1849. Landowners began to look at ways of linking smaller towns to his line, and moves to build a branch line to the ancient Dartmoor town of Moretonhampstead began. Promoters held a meeting at the Globe Hotel in Exmouth on 18 September 1861 and eventually formed the Moretonhampstead & South Devon Railway Company.

The easternmost mile of the granite railroad being used for the new steam line and it was therefore cut back from the canal terminus.

Although by then the tramway was disused, the landowner, the Duke of Somerset, insisted that new interchange sidings between the old and new lines were created a mile south of Bovey Tracey, complete with a crane for lifting blocks of granite, but it was probably never used.

The duke saw the opportunity to rid himself of both the canal and granite tramway

and sold them to the new railway company.

Early hopes that the 12¼-mile steam line would encourage businessmen and middle-class commuters to settle in Moretonhampstead quickly proved ill-founded as Torquay proved more attractive.

The Moretonhampstead branch quickly settled into the daily routine of a typical country branch. When the Great Western Railway took over the branch, it also bought the Stover Canal for £2800.

The branch's three return daily passenger workings increased to five by the end of Victorian times, and tourist numbers were considered sufficient for a private operator to lay on a horsebus to connect Moretonhampstead to the isolated moorland town of Chagford. In April 1906 the GWR introduced a motor bus service between the two, ironic in view of the fact that the original promoters of the branch had intended to extend it to Chagford, which ended up never being served directly by a railway.

The granite tramway had, by comparison, never carried passengers, but around 1905 a scheme to electrify the line and run a frequent tram service was mooted. A small power station was built for it, but the scheme came to nothing. The power station was used by Bovey's clay potteries until it fell into ruin.

The steam branch had intermediate stations at Lustleigh, Bovey Tracey, Chudleigh Road (later renamed Heathfield)

and Teigngrace Halt. Eager to foster 'leisure travel' the GWR bought the luxurious Edwardian home of Lord Hambleton, one of its directors, in 1929 and turned it into the prestigious Manor House Hotel on the lines of Gleneagles in Scotland. One of the more famous guests was Hitler's ambassador Joachim von Ribbentrop.

The 1930s saw branch trains peak at 10 per day and new halts were added at Brimley and Hawkmoor. Lustleigh station was chosen for scenes in a 1931 film version of Sir Arthur Conan Doyle's Sherlock Holmes classic *The Hound of the Baskervilles*, and on 1 December 1937, King George VI visited Moretonhampstead by train.

In 1936, a Mr Jeffrys-Jones presented a section of stone rail from the old granite tramway to the Science Museum, probably for use in an exhibition which told the story of early trackwork.

The growth in car ownership accompanied the postwar decline in the fortunes of the Moretonhampstead branch, and by 1958, most of its passenger services were running empty. Among the locomotives which worked the final passenger services on the branch, on 28 February 1959, was Collett 0-4-2T No 1466, now preserved at Didcot Railway Centre.

Despite the patchy custom, much local fury was vented at the withdrawal of passenger trains, as branch line closures were still a comparatively rare occurrence right up to the days of Dr Beeching and his infamous axe. ➤

The top lock on the Stover Canal at Teigngrace, still in water at this point.

The L-shaped section of the granite block is still visible after nearly two centuries.

Local councillors refused to accept that it really was the end of public transport on the line, and those who opposed the withdrawal of the passenger trains pointed out that British Railways' losses incurred in providing them were only slightly more than £17,000 per annum and great savings could be made by rationalising the infrastructure and introducing diesel railcars and multiple units.

Around this time the young founders of the Bluebell Railway in Sussex had attracted much nationwide publicity over their success in taking over part of a line closed by BR, and history shows that their sterling efforts were to influence events in other areas.

Launching a campaign for the reintroduction of passenger trains to Moretonhampstead, the South Devon Railway Society was formed by the Rector of Teigngrace (where the parish church was built by the Templers with their wealth from the granite quarries), Canon OM Jones and Torquay enthusiast EG Parrott, and on 6 June 1960 a Paignton-Moretonhampstead special, 'The Heart of Devon Rambler' was run, carrying more than 200 people. Shortly afterwards, the society leased Teigngrace Halt as its headquarters.

However, despite the running of a final excursion, the `South Devon Phoenix,' which generated much publicity for the cause, the arguments fell on unsympathetic ears and passenger services never returned to Moretonhampstead.

The line north of Bovey Tracey was closed to freight from 6 April 1964, following the granite tramway into oblivion. The branch was again cut back in 1970, as far as Heathfield, which was kept open to serve a Gulf Oil terminal built in 1966 in addition to ball clay traffic and other goods. The truncated branch was also used for stabling the Royal Train.

Freight declined during the 1990s to the point where the branch was merely 'retained' by Railtrack, but a weekly clay working resumed at the end of the decade.

At the time of writing, 2009, the condition of the surviving part of the branch shows that there has been no traffic for many years. It may be retained as part of the national network, but Mother Nature cares nothing for such designations, and the line is smothered by vegetation.

The South Devon Railway Society was not exactly thwarted in its aims of starting its own passenger services, even though it had to abandon all hope of reviving the Moretonhampstead line. One of the principal reasons was that the branch was unlikely to be closed completely and would still be needed for goods trains.

So members' attention was switched to other redundant branch lines in the locality which could not only be saved but retained as a showcase for heritage traction in a land which would soon be bereft of steam.

Members gave serious consideration to the GWR South Brent-Kingsbridge branch which largely followed the course of the wooded valley of the River Avon and which would undoubtedly have quickly become one of the finest British heritage lines of all had it been preserved. However, contractors had begun dismantling it on the same evening that local council support for its revival had been won.

Separate moves evolved out of the society initiative as a third branch was considered. On 29 September 1962, the *Western Morning News* reported that private plans were afoot to reopen the Totnes-Ashburton branch, which had just closed to freight, passenger services having ended on 1 November 1958.

Lilies adorn the water which has formed a pool in Haytor Quarry, from where granite blocks were carried out by the tramway.

Founders Bob Saunders and Peter Stedman brought together a group of businessmen to reopen the line to passengers and run it on a commercial basis as a tourist attraction. The Dart Valley Light Railway Company Limited was set up to buy the line and acquire suitable locomotives.

Sadly, while the DVR succeeded in reopening Totnes-Buckfastleigh as an attraction for summer tourists, it failed to persuade the Ministry of Transport from taking the top portion, the stretch from Buckfastleigh to Ashburton, as a route for the A38 trunk road scheme of the early 1970s.

Reopening the line in 1969 as a tourist attraction was an overnight success, but the railway world was stunned in 1971 when the company announced plans to buy the Paignton-Kingswear line from BR after it too had been identified for closure. Therein the seeds were sown for what was to become one of the country's most popular heritage lines, today's Paignton & Dartmouth Steam Railway.

The DVR's supporting association took over the Buckfastleigh line in the early 90s and later bought it, rebranding it the South Devon Railway, and its success has also grown steadily over the years. However, both of these superb attractions can trace a lineage back to the granite tramway via the Moretonhampstead line and the efforts to keep it open.

Around the start of the new millennium, plans were made to rebuild another historic transport artery, the Stover Canal, which was inherited from the GWR by British Railways.

Following the purchase of the canal, the GWR leased it in 1893 to Watts & Co for 21 years and also ran its own barges along it. Ball clay, coal and builders' materials were the main sources of freight, as the canal could offer the unrivalled advantage of carrying materials from the clay pit to the port of Teignmouth. However, lorry transport of dehydrated and powdered clay proved more attractive and the canal was basically disused by 1939, the GWR closing the navigation in 1943 and freeing itself of any obligation to maintain it.

In September 1999, the Stover Canal Society was formed with the aim of restoring the waterway as a major leisure amenity for the area. Members of the Waterways Recovery Group, an offshoot of the Inland Waterways Association, carried out significant clearance during a work camp on the canal in 2000.

Restoration is seen as possible; all five lock chambers are still in existence but new gates will be needed and the single major obstruction is a culvert at Lock 2 where the canal is crossed by the truncated Moretonhampstead branch.

The society sees a restored Stover Canal as having huge potential for boating, angling, and wildlife.

As such it would enhance the appeal of the 18-mile Templer Way long-distance footpath.

Taking its name from the family which built the canal and granite railway, the path runs from Haytor Rocks, largely follows the line of the old granite tramway through Heathfield. It passes through the outskirts of Bovey Tracey and Liverton before entering Stover Country Park, the landscaped grounds of James Templer's Stover House, which is now a girl's school.

The park is centred around a giant ornamental lake and, home to many species of waterfowl and dragonflies, and is now a Site of Special Scientific Interest. A waymarked heritage trail follows a circular tour around the Stover Estate, taking in the northern canal basin at Ventiford, running alongside the largely dried-up bed of the waterway and passing into Newton Abbot and along the south shore of the Teign estuary to Shaldon and Teignmouth.

The tramway itself is now a Scheduled Ancient Monument and in recent times efforts have been made to maintain it as such. It is clearly visible for long distances and provided an attractive and fascinating route for ramblers.

The Haytor rocks and quarries are protected from development and disturbance as a Site of Special Scientific Interest, and, surprisingly missed by the many coachloads of visitors who come to climb Haytor before passing on to the teashops of Widecombe-in-the-Moor, Uncle Tom Cobley and all, are one of the most secluded and beautiful parts of Dartmoor National Park. Of course, the best way to reach the quarries is via the tramway!

*Pictures by Robin Jones ■

London Bridge around 1900, when buses were hauled by horses, just like the wagons on the tramway which carried the blocks to build it.

Heathfield was the junction of the Moretonhampstead line, which superseded the Haytor Granite Tramway, and the Teign Valley route to Exeter – which provided a ready diversion in case of blockages on Brunel's main line such as storm surges over the Dawlish sea wall, and accordingly many believe it should have been retained. On 7 June 1958, trains for Paignton, Exeter via the Teign Valley line and Moretonhampstead wait to depart. PETER W GRAY

A cog in the system

Rack and pinion railways are commonplace in the Swiss Alps and present in other mountainous regions around the world, and yet there is just one in the United Kingdom. Accordingly, the Snowdon Mountain Railway, which runs up to the roof of Wales and operates in some of the harshest weather conditions in Britain, qualifies for a place in this book.

The uniqueness of rack railways in Britain is ironic, because we invented them!

The use of a toothed rail and cog fitted to the train to improve adhesion on tracks was the brainchild of Cornishman Richard Trevithick, who invented the world's first railway locomotives. He was concerned that the friction of metal wheels on metal rails would be too low for a substantial weight to be pulled without the engine slipping, so he built his first experimental locomotives with teeth on the wheels on one side that engaged in teeth on the corresponding rails. The system was found to be unnecessary on gentle gradients, but the concept had been introduced.

Not only was this a British first, but the first cog railway in the world was not built to climb dizzy heights in Switzerland or Austria to appreciate chocolate box views, but to serve heavy industry in Yorkshire.

The Middleton Railway, which has operated on the outskirts of Leeds since 1758, and which in 1960 became one of Britain's first volunteer-run heritage lines, installed a rack and pinion system in 1812 when it upgraded from horsepower to steam traction.

The system had been designed and patented by John Blenkinsop in 1811, following on from Trevithick's ideas; and what is claimed to be the world's first commercial steam locomotive, *The Salamanca*, ran along it in 1812. The weight and friction needed to be kept low to stop the locomotive breaking the brittle cast iron rails.

Again, for the first mountain cog railway, we must look not to the continent, but to the USA. It was in 1868 that the Mount Washington Cog Railway in the state of New Hampshire carried its first fare-paying passengers in 1868. The line, designed by Sylvester Marsh, used a central rack system whereby at least two teeth in

the cog on the locomotive are engaged with it at all times. It was extended to the summit of Mount Washington in 1869.

The first mountain rack railway in Europe was the Vitznau-Rigi-Bahn on Mount Rigi in Switzerland, which opened in 1871 and like the Mount Washington line, is still operating today.

It employs the Riggenbach rack system designed by Marsh's contemporary Niklaus Riggenbach working at about the same time as, but independently from Marsh. After Riggenbach was granted a French patent in 1863 and sought investors for a line in Europe, the Swiss consul to the USA visited the Mount Washington Cog Railway and came back with glowing reports. Accordingly, the Swiss government commissioned Riggenbach to build a rack railway up Rigi Mountain.

Several different types of rack or cog systems followed in the wake of the success of these two. The one that chiefly concerns us here was designed by Swiss locomotive engineer Roman Abt, who was employed by Riggenbach at his rack locomotive company. ➤

Snowdon Mountain Railway rack wheel on display at Llanberis. AM HURRALL

A section of the line near Waterfall showing the rack rail. AM HURRALL

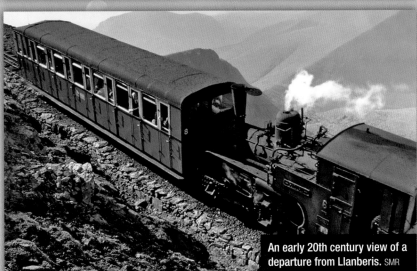

An early 20th century view of a departure from Llanberis. SMR

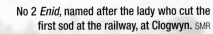

No 2 *Enid*, named after the lady who cut the first sod at the railway, at Clogwyn. SMR

A packed train in the line's early days. SMR

Abt came up with a new rack system that was cheaper to build than Riggenbach's, and had simpler pointwork.

His system was solid bars with vertical teeth machined into them. Two or three of these bars are mounted centrally between the rails, with the teeth offset. The use of multiple bars with offset teeth ensures that the pinions on the locomotive driving wheels are constantly engaged with the rack, and the pinion wheels can be mounted on the same axle as the rail wheels.

The most distinctive feature of rack railway steam locomotives is that they are built with their boilers, cab and general superstructure tilted forward at an angle.

Steam engines can operate only when the boiler is level, because it needs water to cover the boiler tubes and firebox sheets at all times.

Such locomotives often cannot function on level track, and so the whole railway, including sheds and workshops, must be laid on a gradient. That is a prime reason why many continental rack railways have been electrified, as diesel and electric locomotives do not have the same problem.

Another way in which rack railways differ greatly from conventional lines is that the locomotives always push the carriages, for reasons of safety. The engines are fitted with powerful brakes that grip the rack rail solidly. Some have automatic brakes that apply if the speed gets too high, preventing runaways.

The carriages are often left uncoupled to the locomotive: gravity will always push the vehicle down against the locomotive.

The idea of a railway running to the summit of Mount Snowdon, the highest peak in England and Wales, was first proposed in 1869, as more and more tourists discovered the delights of Snowdonia, arriving at Llanberis from Caernarfon via a branch of the London & North Western Railway to take the mountain path. However, the scheme fizzled out after the landowner decided it would ruin the view.

When the 1ft 11½ gauge North Wales Narrow Gauge Railways (later the Welsh Highland Railway) was laid past the western side of Snowdon, and plans to build a mountain railway from its station at Rhyd Ddu were made, Llanberis traders feared that their town would lose out big time.

The roof of Wales: No 6 Padarn with a train at Summit Low. SMR

The railway in winter. SMR

As a counter measure, the Snowdon Mountain Tramway and Hotel Company was formed to build the railway, without an Act of Parliament, as it was to be laid entirely on private land without any compulsory purchase necessary.

The first sod was cut in December 1894 by Enid Assheton-Smith, a member of the landowner's family, and February 1896, at a cost of £63,800. It used the Abt rack system, and involved two large viaducts being built between Llanberis and Waterfall.

The 2ft 7½in gauge railway was built to a total length of four miles 1188 yards, with an average gradient of 1-in-7.86 as it rises from 353ft above sea level at Llanberis to 3493ft at Summit station, offering stunning views of the glaciated landscape over almost every inch of the way. The steepest gradient on the route is 1-in-5.5.

As built, there were seven stations, beginning with the terminus at Llanberis, where the company offices, locomotive shed and workshops are sited.

The first station up the mountain, Waterfall, was built to allow visitors to ride on the train to travel to see a spectacular waterfall nearby, but it is now closed.

Hebron station at 1069ft was named after the nearby Hebron chapel and Halfway station at 1641ft is as its name implies. Further up, the line runs to Rocky Valley Halt and then reaches Clogwyn station at 2556ft, which overlooks the Llanberis Pass and the Clogwyn Du'r Arddu cliffs. The wind speed is measured at Clogwyn station to check whether it is safe for trains to proceed to the summit; if not, they stop at Rocky Valley Halt. ➤

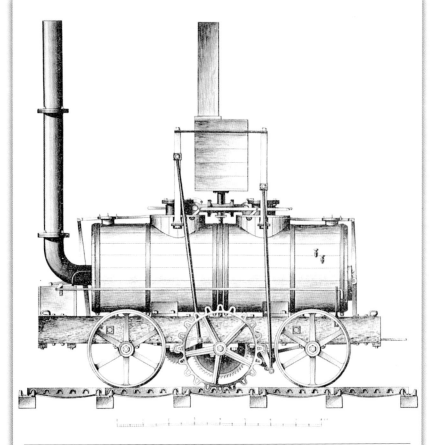

World first: *The Salamanca*, built in 1812 by Matthew Murray of Holbeck for the edge railed Middleton Railway, was a rack and pinion locomotive using John Blenkinsop's patented design for rack propulsion. A single rack ran outside the tracks and was engaged by a large cogwheel on the left side of the locomotive. The engine was destroyed six years later when its boiler exploded. THE MECHANIC'S MAGAZINE, 1829

Summit station is just 68ft below the 3560ft mountain peak.

While Britain led the world in terms of locomotive manufacture, only the Swiss had experience building rack locomotives, so the Swiss Locomotive and Machine Works of Winterthur was awarded the contract to build the first five Snowdon engines.

All of them are 0-4-2Ts, Nos 1 to 3 were used in building the line. During 1922/23, three more engines were ordered from SLM, becoming Nos 6-8.

The first train physically reached the summit in January 1896, but due to much of the line's infrastructure not being complete, it was not opened until Easter 1896.

The line was officially opened on Monday 6 April, and two trains ran up to the summit.

On the first return trip down the mountain, locomotive No 1 *Ladas* with two carriages lost the rack and ran out of control. The locomotive derailed and tumbled down the mountainside to its destruction.

A passenger, Ellis Griffith Roberts of Llanberis, died from loss of blood after jumping from his carriage. The second downward train hauled by No 2 *Enid* then hit the carriages of the first, but there were no more fatalities.

An inquiry ruled that the cause of the accident was post-construction settlement, compounded by excess speed caused by the weight of the train. Henceforth, the maximum allowed train weight was reduced to the equivalent of one-and-a-half carriages. As a result, lighter carriages were built to make up two-carriage trains.

Furthermore, a gripper system was installed to boost adhesion on the rack. On the steeper sections of the line, gripper rails are fixed to either side of the rack rail in the form of an inverted 'L' cross section. A gripper is fitted to each locomotive, which fits around the gripper rails and holds the locomotive to the rails and prevents the pinion working itself free from the rack. Snowdon is the only Abt rack railways to use a gripper system, although the feature is common on other rack systems.

The railway reopened on 9 April 1897, and there was no repeat of the calamity.

The railway took off as a major tourist attraction, especially among people who had never visited the continent and were amazed by the sight of the tilting locomotives.

In 1935, a new summit station was built. It was designed by Sir William Clough-Ellis, who had created the wonderful Italianate village of Portmeirion near Porthmadog and which shot to fame in the 60s as the setting for the cult TV spy series *The Prisoner.*

However, in later years, its grim functionality came to be widely criticised as one of the architect's less fine moments, and Prince Charles famously described it as 'the highest slum in Wales'.

Services were partly disrupted by World War Two, and when they resumed afterwards, a national shortage of coal led to old army boots being burned in the locomotive fireboxes.

British Railways closed the Llanberis-Caernarfon branch to passengers in 1962, leaving the mountain railway without a nearby station on the national rail network for the first time.

A share issue made in 1985 raised money to buy the line's first two diesel locomotives.

Between 1986 and 1992, four Hunslet diesel locomotives were built specially for the railway, and became Nos 9-12. In 1995, the diesels were followed by three identical railcars built by HPE Tredegar Ltd and

designed to run as either two- or three-car multiple units.

Service trains depart from Llanberis at regular intervals, up to every 30 minutes at busy times, and in the peak summer season are often sold out.

The first train of the day is the works train, which takes supplies, including drinking water and fuel for the generator, to the summit, as well as provisions for the café at Halfway, and also carries the permanent way maintenance gang.

In 2006, the offending summit café was demolished and fundraising started for a state-of-the-art replacement, which was officially opened on 12 June in 2009 by Welsh First Minister Rhodri Morgan. It was named Hafod Eryri, Welsh for 'high residence of Snowdonia' and cost a total of £8.4-million, mostly financed by grant aid.

The railway played a part in its construction, by transporting much of the building materials to the summit – and therefore running real freight trains in the process. In the formative years, it had been hoped that the railway might have attracted some agricultural traffic as well as passengers.

The railway was immortalised by the Rev Wilbert Awdry in his Thomas the Tank Engine series of books. It is the inspiration for the Culdee Fell Railway, a fictional cog railway on the Island of Sodor, in the book *Mountain Engines.*

*For details of train times or to make advance bookings, telephone 0871 720 0033. ∎

The route at Clogwyn follows a ridge and offers breathtaking panoramas of the glaciated landscape. SMR

The Mount Washington Cog Railway. In recent years, long-serving Snowdon Mountain Railway engineer Nigel Day has been helping its US counterpart with improvements to locomotive performance and experiments on the conversion of steam locomotives to oil firing. MWCR

'Services were partly disrupted by World War Two, and when they resumed afterwards, a national shortage of coal led to old army boots being burned in the locomotive fireboxes.'

The 6ft 6¾in broad gauge Cairngorm Mountain Railway which opened in 2001 is the highest railway in the United Kingdom, but is a cable-operated funicular line, not a rack railway like Snowdon. FRASER ANDERSON

The railway is dwarfed by the landscape as it climbs towards the summit. SMR

Tunnelling through fairyland

The romantic Cornish island of St Michaels Mount regularly featured in the Great Western Railway's summer holiday guide – which did not mention that it had a secret line of its own.

The fairytale Cornish island of St Michael's Mount has been a source of myths and legends since time immemorial. Its greatest secret, however, is a feature not of the imagination, but of technology.

The wooded rocky outcrop with its romantic castle, miniature harbour and fishing village, and connected to the mainland at low tide by a granite causeway, is the centrepiece of one of the most romantic seascapes in Britain, on which delights passengers on board main line trains approaching Penzance as soon as the coast breaks into view.

Historians believe that the island was Ictis, the place where the great seafarers of the ancient world, the Phoenicians, traded in tin from Cornish mines in the Iron Age.

Various tales have linked it with the archangel Michael and a giant called Cormoran who later perished at the hands of Jack the Giant Killer.

The island also features heavily in the legends of the lost kingdom of Lyonesse, which stretched from Land's End to the Isles of Scilly and which was destroyed in a night by a massive earthquake, caused by Merlin the magician in revenge for the death of King Arthur.

The island's Cornish name means 'hoar rock in the wood' suggesting that it once lay several miles from the coast and was surrounded by trees; there is much truth in this, as the stumps of a prehistoric forest can sometimes be glimpsed at low tide.

The chronicler John of Worcester wrote that the now-submerged land fell beneath the waves in a great storm of November 1099, but science disagrees, for the stumps have been carbon dated to 1700BC, before recorded history began in Cornwall.

A group of monks from Mont St Michel in Normandy – almost a carbon copy of St Michael's Mount, as it is also a fortified isle linked to the coast by a tidal causeway were given the Cornish island in the 11th century and built a Benedictine priory on its summit. Subsequently, centuries before Cornwall became Britain's favourite summer holiday destination, with much help from the Great

Western Railway (which had a station opposite the isle at Marazion, where redundant Pullman cars were later sited as camping coaches), St Michael's Mount attracted tourists in the form of pilgrims to the priory.

This ecclesiastical settlement survived until Henry VIII fell out with Rome over his divorce from his first wife, and dissolved the monasteries.

The remains of the island priory were later rebuilt into a castle. In 1588, the first beacon to warn of the coming Spanish Armada was lit there.

In 1659, St Michael's Mount was sold to Colonel John St Aubyn, who turned the castle into his family's home, and whose descendant, Lord St Levan, gave the island to the National Trust in 1954 and now hordes of tourists rather than pilgrims make the journey to the little harbour each year, either by boat or across the causeway, climbing steps to the medieval castle to inspect the plaster reliefs of hunting scenes in the Chevy Chase Room (the former refectory), the armoury and the fine furniture of the Blue Drawing Room. ➤

Above: **The short length of 2ft 5in gauge rail set in the island quay is the only part of the railway that the public regularly see.** ROBIN JONES

Right: **A cargo of old newspapers is received at harbour station.** ROBIN JONES

Below right: **The buffer stop at the harbour station ensures that the train never comes into contact with passers-by on the quayside.** ROBIN JONES

Below: **Boatman Dave Ladner unloading the train at the harbour station, which is housed in a metal cage.** ROBIN JONES

The railway tunnel inside the hill.

Emerging from the darkness:
the tunnel ends at the 'tramyard.'

The entrance from the quayside
to the 'tramyard.' ALL ROBIN JONES

The winding gear at
the summit. ROBIN JONES

Waiting for the train at the
'pantry' station. ROBIN JONES

The head of the family is still the island's 'lord'. The family live in the Victorian wing of the castle which was built between 1873 and 1878.

However, every fairytale castle should have a dark secret, and very few of the 200,000 or so annual visitors ever stumble across it.

Even less believe that it has its own working railway; no, not a model, nor a pleasure line, a toy or a gimmick, but a real working freight-carrying operation, one which was never threatened by the Beeching Axe (he probably never knew it was there) never came into the ownership of British Rail, and yet has successfully operated almost every day since it was built.

It is a unique 2ft 5in gauge cable-operated incline line, which is around an eighth of a mile in length, and runs through the middle of the hill on which the castle is built.

Once operated at speeds of up to 40mph, it boasts a slope of 1-in-1.9 as it ascends 174ft from bottom to top.

Its bottom station lies next to the island's quayside, from where supplies for the castle are loaded into a wagon. Its top station is a room in the castle's kitchen pantry – and the run between the two is non-stop!

The only public clue to the existence of the railway is the short length of rail laid tramway-style on the quayside beyond a set of wooden double doors between the harbourside cottages that lead to its base station, known as the 'tramyard' and nowadays concealed in a steel cage for security.

Apart from one section where tunnelling was essential, the railway was constructed in 1901 by local miners using a 'cut and cover' method with a brick arch to conceal it from view. It replaced the packhorses which previously hauled provisions up the hill.

Cornwall is famous for its mining traditions – Richard Trevithick, who invented the world's first railway engine – came from a local mine engineering background – and the miner's practice of spiking the rails directly onto the rock face was used for much of its length. Some of the original rails were still in place and in regular use a century later.

The line has a single item of rolling stock – a wagon which is hauled up and down the line by a cable connected to an electric-operated winding drum at the summit station.

Alongside the 'tramyard' stands the engine house, which contains the old winding machinery which became redundant when health and safety regulations forced the line's 'modernisation' in 1988. As designed, the winding gear at the bottom of the line hauled the cable over a pulley at the top.

This railway never saw steam traction. Power was originally supplied by a gas engine, but a Ruston petrol engine replaced it in the 1920s. When an 11,000-volt power cable supplying the island from the mainland was installed in 1951, this engine was in turn replaced by a Crompton Parkinson motor.

Inside the engine house, a system was operated whereby white marks had to line up on each of three giant cog wheels on the winding gear in the base station to indicate that the brake should be applied; if a miscalculation was made or there was a lack of concentration, gravity would take its course and the wagon would end up wherever the maximum slack allowed.

Prior to the 1988 upgrading, there had been several accidents on the railway, some which led to the wagon overshooting the buffer stops, smashing through the quayside wall... and ending up in the sea.

Luckily, there were never any injuries, but in these safety-conscious days, the possibility of the wagon smashing through the tramyard doors into passing holidaymakers has to be eradicated.

From the harbour station, where the wagon is unloaded and loaded, the line passes from daylight into the tunnel which is 5ft wide and 7ft tall and starts its ascent to the summit on a slight curve.

The tunnel begins on a slope of 1-in-14, increasing to 1-in-4 over the first 250ft, and is well lit by electric lamps at regular intervals.

An upturn after this first stage takes the line up a 1-in-3 gradient for a distance of 160ft before reaching a 120ft section on a level of 1-in-1.9.

View of St. Michael's Mount showing its castle, the harbour and village. The hand-coloured postcard dates from 1900, shortly before the island's secret railway was built. ROBIN JONES COLLECTION

'Even less believe that it has its own working railway: no, not a model, nor a pleasure line, a toy or a gimmick, but a real working freight-carrying operation…'

Nearing the summit, the roof height diminishes to 6ft where the tunnel has been cut through the granite.

The journey originally ended next to the top station, known as the 'coal station'. It was situated alongside the boiler house just below the kitchens. The boiler house provides heating for the castle, but coal is no longer ferried by the railway as the boiler is now oil fired. However, the oil is piped through the tunnel.

At the 'coal station', supplies were unloaded with the wagon held by the cable in near-vertical position on the 1-in-1.9 slope. Commodities were often unloaded by means of a winch affixed to the adjacent wall of the castle, hoisted over an adjacent roof and lowered through holes in the ceilings of two storerooms serving the castle kitchens, which are off limits to the public.

However, the 1988 improvements saw the line extended to a new terminus about 20ft further up from the 'coal station', in what once served as a pantry for the kitchen. The summit station, now referred to as the 'pantry', allows the wagon to be unloaded almost on the level.

Boatman Dave Ladner, who was operating the railway from its harbour station when I

visited the line, said: "The last incident happened when the wagon came down carrying a load of ashes. By the time we stopped it, it had reached the doors to the harbour.

"There are three marks on the winding mechanism which had to be lined up. When that happened, if you did not slam the brake on, the wagon ended up in the harbour.

"Incidents used to happen on a regular basis until alterations were made to the line."

Bob Hunt, head guide at the castle in the late 1990s, enjoyed an early introduction to driving trains. Both his grandfathers were GWR drivers, one at Swindon, the other at Newton Abbot. At the age of 12, however, when a relative worked at the giant Penlee Quarries which dominate the coastline south of Newlyn, he and a friend would sneak inside after dark with the keys to one of the site's narrow-gauge diesel locomotives – and drive it up and down the running line. Bob now drives a train quite legally – from the control panel in the 'pantry' next to the castle kitchen.

"The wagon used to travel at speeds of up to 40mph," he recalled. "It used to come whistling down the incline and by the time it reached the bottom it had created such a build-up of air pressure that it cleaned the tunnel out."

Before World War Two, serious consideration was given to converting the line for passenger use, but no action was taken.

However, Bob explained: "At one time seasonal staff at the castle had a tradition of riding inside the wagon as a dare at least once during their six-month summer spell, but it was against the rules even in those days.

"Riding inside the wagon made your ears pop as you went down. At the bottom end of the tunnel you'd think that it was never going to stop, and then suddenly the brake would go on."

Since the modifications were made, the train now takes a more modest 2mins 35secs to make the journey at a more controlled speed – and joyriding is definitely out.

The sole wagon is not the original; it is the latest of several which have been used in succession on the line during its history, but sadly, none have made it into preservation!

So St Michael's Mount is a prime example of one of the most contorted uses of the railway concept in the British Isles. Ingenious in its simplicity, the existence of the railway adds to the aura of magic about the island.

The National Trust does not permit public access to the railway. ∎

The Steam Elephant lines up with the *Puffing Billy* replica.
BEAMISH

The world's first trunk railway!

The steam engine replaced equine haulage on early railways, and appropriately soon became known as the iron horse. However, in those embryonic days of locomotive development, there was an even mightier and bulkier beast: the Steam Elephant. Using the sketchiest surviving information, Beamish Museum in County Durham managed to bring one of these mammoths back from extinction.

In 2009, steam hit the headlines big time with the main line debut of *Tornado*, the 50th member of the otherwise extinct class of Peppercorn A1 Pacifics, which had been built from scratch by the A1 Steam Locomotive Trust over 18 years.

However, building new steam locomotives to fill missing gaps in British railway heritage was by no means new. Beamish – The North of England Open Air Museum in County Durham – constructed a replica of *Locomotion No 1* in 1975. The original was supplied by Robert Stephenson to haul trains on the world's first passenger-carrying steam railway, the Stockton & Darlington Railway, in 1825. While the original survives, in the Head of Steam museum at Darlington's

North Road station, the Beamish replica is fully operational.

Locomotion No1 is well known, well documented and world famous as a landmark in transport engineering. Not only that, but also anyone wishing to build a copy of it has only to inspect the original for starters.

The years of early locomotive development is akin to the Dark Ages, those shadowy centuries when Romano-British rule in England and Wales gave way to Saxon kingdoms. Back in the early 1800s, there were, of course, no railway magazines, no lineside enthusiasts to take photographs, and few newspapers which would have documented every new locomotive design. Richard Trevithick gave his first public

demonstration of a steam locomotive in 1804, but despite subsequent designs, including *Catch-me-who-can*, which hauled the world's first self-propelled passenger train in London four years later, there were few takers, and lack of interest forced him to seek other pursuits.

His invention might not have been an overnight success, but it was certainly not forgotten. Horse traction still reigned supreme, that is, until unduly large numbers were taken overseas for use by the British army in the Napoleonic Wars. The shortage of horses posed a particular problem in the coalfields of the north-east, and colliery owners began by necessity to look at fresh forms of haulage.

In 1812, the Middleton Railway became the first commercial railway to successfully use steam locomotives. Colliery manager John Blenkinsop approached Matthew Murray of Fenton, Murray and Wood in Holbeck, Leeds, to produce one, and he came up with a locomotive based on Catch-me-who-can, called Salamanca. William Hedley and Timothy Hackworth's *Puffing Billy* from 1813 survives at the Science Museum, while Beamish created a working replica in 2005. Another local engineer, William Chapman, who had a rope works at Willington, built chain-drive locomotives in 1813, and the following year, George Stephenson finished his first locomotive.

There were undoubtedly more designs, many of which never left the drawing board. Some were built, only to disappear in the mists of time because complete records were either not kept or have not survived.

It is suggested that a second Trevithick locomotive existed in the north east after the one built at Gateshead for Wylam Colliery owner Christopher Blackett. One version of this story places the locomotive at Chapman's works.

An account book in the possession of Beamish Museum records a payment on 20 June 1815 for 'six waggon wheels for locomotive' and a kit of locomotive parts.

Further research found evidence that this 'mystery' locomotive underwent trials at Washington, while an oil painting – the earliest known one of a steam locomotive – showed it hauling chaldron wagons at Wallsend. An illustration of the locomotive had first come to modern attention in 1931

The Steam Elephant may itself be no oil painting, and is certainly not as aesthetically pleasing as *Flying Scotsman*, *Mallard* or the restreamlined *Duchess of Hamilton*. However, it has been recreated largely from observations of an oil painting!

when it was wrongly assumed to be the work of George Stephenson.

Built by Hawks and Company of Gateshead, a forgotten firm of locomotive builders, it was a Steam Elephant: the locomotive that time forgot.

It was designed by Chapman for mining engineer John Buddle, nicknamed 'King of the Coal Trade' in the north east, who had succeeded his father as manager at Wallsend Colliery in 1806 and introduced the safety lamp invented by Humphry Davy there.

The Steam Elephant was a six-wheeled locomotive of approximately standard gauge with a centre-flue boiler having two vertical cylinders set into its top centreline. The cylinders drove slidebar-mounted beams which turned crankshafts driving the axles through reduction gears between the frames.

It had a tall, tapering chimney, probably its most visually distinctive feature. It weighed about 7.5 tons and had a top speed of around 4.5mph.

The water for the boiler was pre-heated before it was pumped into the boiler in a jacket placed around the bottom of the chimney. This method not only saved fuel but also stopped the problems caused by pumping cold water straight into a hot boiler. ➤

The centrepiece of the Pockerley Waggonway at Beamish Museum is this replica 1825 engine shed, which houses the museum's early locomotive replicas, including the Steam Elephant (centre), with *Puffing Billy* (left) and *Locomotion No 1* (right). The creation of such replicas allows the public to see them in a recreated working environment, and Beamish has established itself as a world leader in this field. BEAMISH

'The Steam Elephant is certainly a jumbo-sized oddity by the standards of today's fleet of heritage steam locomotives'

Rear view of the Steam Elephant and its firebox. BEAMISH

It appears that it was at first unsuccessful at Wallsend, probably due to lack of adhesion on the wooden rails there; but once iron rails were introduced, it worked until at least the mid-1820s. Some evidence suggests that it was rebuilt for the Hetton collieries and worked there for another 10 years, possibly named Fox. Contemporary reports imply that there may have been more than one Steam Elephant working at Wallsend.

Once the researchers at Beamish had established the identity of the mystery locomotive, a decision was taken to attempt the impossible: using just the oil painting and four other contemporary pictures, knowledge of early locomotives, the contemporary Puffing Billy and models of other engines of the day, a new full-size Steam Elephant was to be built.

The £360,000 project was undertaken by Jim Rees, keeper of industry at the museum and locomotive driver on its Pockerley Waggonway early railways demonstration lines, and Andy Guy, a library researcher.

They produced a set of engineering drawings and, in October 1999, started building the Elephant. Overall, the project took six years, with final assembly being undertaken by locomotive builder Alan Keef at his workshops in Ross-on-Wye before it was launched in 2002. While the exact gauge of the original Elephant remains unclear, the modern one was built to standard gauge, so it could run on Beamish – and any other railway wishing to hire it, provided they have no bridges to clash with its trunk-like chimney.

The Steam Elephant is certainly a jumbo-sized oddity by the standards of today's fleet of heritage steam locomotives. Its type appears to be very much one of a kind: a very much local though workable design produced at a time when steam locomotive technology was in the early melting pot.

Dating from 1815, it fits almost halfway between Trevithick's first road steam locomotive of 1801 and *Locomotion No 1* in 1825, and offers a valuable insight into the thinking of contemporary designers and builders.

While Chapman's first locomotives hauled themselves along using a chain between the rails, his later locomotives, including the Elephants, used adhesion.

Chapman also invented the bogie, while it was Buddle who first installed metal springs on engines; these two innovations helped shape the future course of steam locomotive technology. However, what part the Elephant played in either of them has long been forgotten. ∎

The Steam Elephant – the first standard gauge steam locomotive to be built in the 21st century – sets off with a train on the Pockerley Waggonway. BEAMISH

The oil painting from 1820 which shows the original Steam Elephant, or one of them, taking a load of chaldron wagons towards the docks at Wallsend. BEAMISH

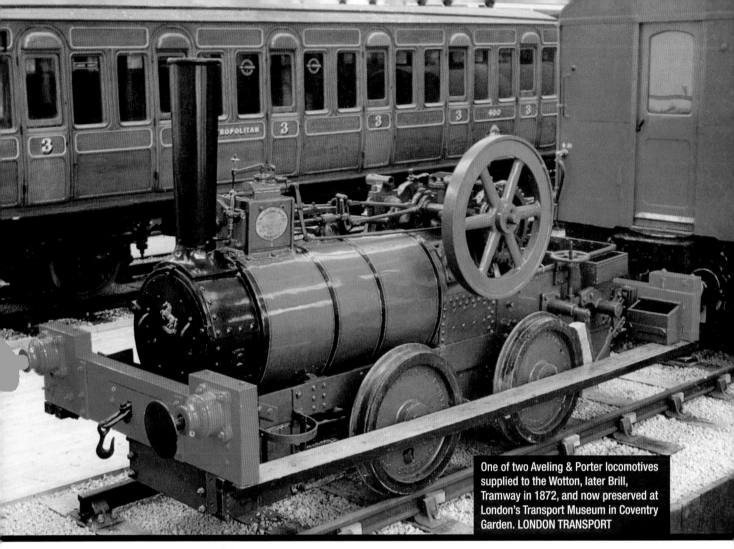

One of two Aveling & Porter locomotives supplied to the Wotton, later Brill, Tramway in 1872, and now preserved at London's Transport Museum in Coventry Garden. LONDON TRANSPORT

Just Brill!

Following on from the pioneer work undertaken by Magnus Volk, London developed a transport system that was the envy of the world, with electrified railways both below and above ground providing a fast and efficient way of transporting millions of people to and from work and the shops. However, the furthest outpost of the London Underground system was, briefly, a remote and eccentric six-and-a-half mile branch that appeared to belong back in the early years of the steam age.

Fifty-one miles from the Baker Street terminus of the Metropolitan Line by train stood the Buckinghamshire village of Brill. Back in the mid-30s, it was the furthest point that you could travel from the capital via London Underground, and the remotest part of the late poet laureate John Betjeman's fabled Metroland, but few ever did.

Those that ventured this far found no sleek tube trains whizzing through tunnels. Instead, Metropolitan Railway steam locomotives hauling trains of vintage wooden carriages back and forth from the junction with the main line at Quainton Road, a route shared by the Met and the Great Central Railway. Before that, the line to Brill had used flywheel-driven locomotives whose appearance had far more in common with traction engines.

The little branch was built by third Duke of Buckingham and Marquess of Chandos, who lived at early 18th-century Wotton House, and who served as chairman of the London & North Western Railway from 1853-61.

Originally known at the Wotton Tramway because of the estate it served, and later known as the Brill Tramway, the duke had it built on his land for agricultural and industrial use between 1870 and 1872. It was also opened as a public railway. ➤

The first section from Quainton Road to Wotton was brought into use on 1 April 1871, and the whole line to Brill completed by summer 1872.

Running from Quainton Road (opened by the Aylesbury & Buckingham Railway in 1868) to Waddesdon (renamed Waddesdon Road in 1922 to distinguish it from Waddesdon Manor on the main line between Aylesbury and Quainton Road), Westcott, Wotton and Wood Siding.

Its western terminus beneath the hill-top village of Brill was 700ft above sea level. At first there was a halt at Church Siding, between Wotton and Wood Siding, at the junction with a spur to Woodham near Kingswood, the site of a coal wharf. A branch line connected the tramway to a brick and tile works.

In its first few months, the tramway was initially operated by horses, and by its own steam locomotives from 1872 until 1906.

The first two locomotives were very unconventional 0-4-0 single-cylinder geared steam locomotives supplied by Aveling & Porter, works numbers 807 and 846, supplied at a cost of £400 each. Each 10-ton locomotive had a single overslung cylinder connected through a countershaft and pinion to further pinions on the axles.

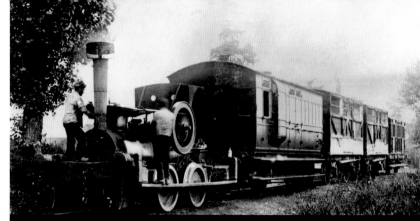

An Aveling & Porter steam engine hauling a passenger train on the Brill Tramway around 1890. LONDON'S TRANSPORT MUSEUM/TRANSPORT FOR LONDON

Their maximum speed was about 8mph.

Both were later sold to Nether Heyford brickworks, near Weedon, Northamptonshire, and which kept them until 1950. No 1 survives in the custody of London's Transport Museum in Covent Garden.

The next two locomotives were supplied by WG Bagnall of Stoke-on-Trent, in the form of 0-4-0 saddle tank *Buckingham*, works number 16 of 1876, and 0-4-0 tank engine *Wotton*, number 120 of 1877. They were unusual in having 'reversed' inside cylinders, which drove the front axle.

The operation of the tramway was at first contracted out, while maintenance work

was undertaken by the duke's staff. Signalling was a primitive affair, but only one engine was in use on the tramway at any one time.

The operating regulations were notably strict: a rule book published in 1873 listed fines which might be levied on staff for misdemeanours, such as: "If the train be late at Quainton Junction in consequence of a late start, the fault of the driver in not having his engine ready, a fine of half a day's pay to be imposed."

A scheme to build an Oxford, Aylesbury & Metropolitan Junction Railway by extending the tramway from Brill to the great university city 10 miles away, were drawn up in 1883, but nothing ever came of it.

In 1888, Parliament approved a similar scheme drawn up by the Oxford & Aylesbury Tramway Company, which took over the running of the tramway in 1894 on the death of the duke. The Oxford terminus would have been near Magdalen Bridge on the edge of the city centre. However, the necessary money could not be raised and the cost of tunnelling beneath 600ft Muswell Hill to the west of Brill would probably have been too much for the company.

Nevertheless, the Oxford & Aylesbury Tramroad Company improved the tramway,

End of the line: Brill station as pictured in 1935. LONDON'S TRANSPORT MUSEUM/TRANSPORT FOR LONDON

Metropolitan A class locomotive No 23 of 1866 at the level crossing at Wood Siding station on the Brill branch, pictured on 21 September 1934, when it was part of the London Underground empire. A guard is operating the crossing gates. LONDON'S TRANSPORT MUSEUM/TRANSPORT FOR LONDON

An early picture of one of the tramway's first locomotives. LONDON'S TRANSPORT MUSEUM/TRANSPORT FOR LONDON

replacing the original light rails laid on longitudinal sleepers with flat-bottomed rails spiked direct to transverse sleepers as well as much of the rolling stock.

Out went the Aveling & Porters, and in came Manning Wardle industrial-type 0-6-0 saddle tanks with inside cylinders, one being replaced by another Manning Wardle in 1899. They were *Earl Temple*, works number 1249 of 1894, *Huddersfield*, works number 616, a second-hand locomotive built 1876, withdrawn 1899 and *Wotton No 2*, works number 1415, built 1899. *Earl Temple* was later renamed *Brill No 1*.

In December 1899, the Metropolitan Railway, which built the first physical link between the tramway and the main line, acquired a lease on the tramway, and brought in new locomotives and rolling stock, but never exercised an option to buy it outright.

Betjeman would later recall fond memories of the tramway during a visit to Quainton Road in 1929. In his 1973 television documentary Metroland, he spoke of watching the Brill branch train depart: "the steam ready to take two or three passengers through oil-lit halts and over level crossings, a rather bumpy journey."

It was in 1933 that the London Passenger Transport Board was formed, taking over all the underground railway companies and unifying them in one body.

Among the board's portfolio was the Metropolitan Railway, and with it was inherited the Brill Tramway.

The mid-30s saw closures of many famous light railways as motor transport rendered them unable to make ends meet, including the Leek & Manifold Valley, the Lynton & Barnstaple and the Welsh Highland,

The Brill Tramway was no exception and on 30 November 1935, it was closed by the board along with all stations beyond Aylesbury, and Quainton Road closed to passengers in 1963.

Metropolitan Railway Manning Wardle locomotive *Brill No 2* on the Brill branch around 1900. LONDON'S TRANSPORT MUSEUM/TRANSPORT FOR LONDON

Nothing remains of the tramway today, apart from privately owned Westcott station, but its route can be seen in a double row of hedges running parallel to the lane to the west of Quainton Road.

Passenger trains on the Great Central route from Marylebone to Nottingham ceased to call at Quainton Road from 1963, and on 3 September 1966, the complete route was closed to passengers apart from services between Nottingham and Rugby which lingered on until 1969.

Meanwhile, the London Railway Preservation Society which had been formed to save locomotives and stock from the steam age before they all disappeared acquired the

use of Quainton Road and its sizeable goods yard as a base. Reforming as the Quainton Railway Society, they set up what is now the Buckinghamshire Railway Centre.

Ironically, over the years two Aveling & Porter locomotives similar to those used on the tramway have been based at the centre at one time or another. In the early 21st century, members built a replica Brill Tramway coach to offer the public rides behind one of them, and plans to relay a mile of the tramway were mooted – the wooden waiting room on platforms 2 and 3 at Quainton Road was once the shelter for passengers waiting for Brill branch trains – but they came to nothing. Yet who knows what might happen one day? ■

Cut down to size!

While an obvious solution to running a railway in places where clearances may be very tight is to choose narrow rather than standard gauge, that option has not always been followed. Standard gauge steam locomotives which are very different in shape and size from their 'normal' counterparts in regular main line service have always been part and parcel of the railway sectors. Here we look at a selection of those still active in the heritage sector today.

In 2009, a unique pair of twins burst on to the preservation scene, for it was the first year that both had been available to run and so they could steam together. They were soon in much demand.

The Bodmin & Wenford Railway is home to *Alfred* and *Judy*, two very unusual standard gauge Bagnall 0-4-0 saddle tanks, so much so that Thomas the Tank engine creator the Rev Wilbert Awdry immortalised them as Bill and Ben in his series of railway stories. As such, they have already appeared at Days out With Thomas weekends at places like the West Somerset Railway and the Tanfield railway.

Their diminutive size all comes down to Brunel's Cornwall Railway, or rather, a bridge built beneath it to access the port of Par.

Par harbour between Fowey and St Austell was built by Joseph Treffry and was first used in 1833, linking to tramways serving his inland copper mines and granite quarries.

In 1860, a connection was made between the harbour's internal railway lines, which were horse worked, and the Cornwall Railway.

In 1881, a new branch line was taken through an 8ft high bridge beneath the Cornish main line to serve a new china clay processing works. Not only was the bridge too low for 'normal' locomotives to run beneath it, but there was a tight 70ft radius curve. Locomotives which could overcome these two obstacles had to be obtained if the line was ever to be worked by steam.

In 1913, a small four-wheel vertical-boiler locomotive built by Sara and Burgess in Penryn arrived in 1912, followed three years later by a more conventional second-hand small Manning Wardle 0-4-0 saddle tank called *Punch*. Another vertical-boilered locomotive, this time built by the Shrewsbury firm of Sentinel and named *Toby* arrived in 1927. Harbour staff also built an engine of their own made from parts of two steam cranes.

None of these really fitted the bill perfectly, so a larger locomotive was ordered from WG Bagnall at a cost of £1200 and delivered in 1937.

To go with the earlier *Punch*, it was named *Judy*, although it did not get its nameplates until 1960. Built as works number 2572, the bespoke locomotive was only 90 inches high, allowing it to pass beneath the low bridge. This reduction in height was facilitated by dropping the cab floor down between the main frames. At 16ft 6in long over headstocks and 7ft 5in wide, Judy's 33in wheels set just 5ft (apart allowed it to negotiate the sharp curve by the Par Moors clay drier.

It was able to haul clay wagons in and out of the harbour complex to St Blazey, allowing them to be taken onwards by conventional locomotives that were registered to run over the national network.

A second one built to virtually the same design followed it to Par in 1954. This one, works number 3058, was named *Alfred* after the manager of the harbour, Alfred Truscott.

Toby was kept as a spare locomotive until it was withdrawn in 1957, while *Judy* ended its working days in 1969 when part of the firebox needed to be renewed, and was kept in the harbour engine shed until 1978. *Alfred*, however, was kept in service until 1977.

Alfred and *Judy* in action on the Tanfield Railway in County Durham on 14 September 2009. BRIAN SHARPE

In 1978, *Judy* was sent to the Wheal Martyn China Clay Museum at St Austell as a static exhibit, and in 2004 handed over to the Cornish Steam Locomotive Preservation Society, which has restored the locomotive at Bodmin with the aid of a Heritage Lottery Fund grant. *Judy* moved under its own power on 31 October 2008 for the first time in nearly 40 years and entered service on the Bodmin & Wenford Railway in April 2009.

Alfred was moved to the Cornish Steam Locomotive Preservation Society's original site at nearby Bugle in 1978 where a vacuum brake was fitted so that it could haul passenger trains over the short-lived Bugle Steam Railway, set up on a disused clay spur off the Newquay branch.

In 1987 the society moved to the Bodmin & Wenford Railway and took *Alfred* with them. In the late 90s it was painted yellow livery, the colour worn by Bill and Ben, but has now been repainted back into the green Port of Par livery to match *Judy*.

In August 2002, it took part in an open day at St Blazey's main line depot and was steamed down the branch to Par harbour for the first time in 25 years. In May 2009 it was taken to Saltash as part of the 150th anniversary of Brunel's Royal Albert Bridge.

Par docks is still rail connected, but the internal system is all but gone. When wagons have to be moved beneath the bridge, tractors subsequently did the job.

Meanwhile, it seems that Bill and Ben, sorry, *Alfred* and *Judy*, will be undertaking nationwide tours of heritage lines every year.

Not all cut-down locomotives or those with a decidedly unconventional appearance were restricted to private industrial lines off the national network.

The Somerset & Dorset Joint Railway employed two low-bodied Sentinel four-wheeled vertical-boilered shunters which had a somewhat bizarre bell-shaped smokebox and boiler cladding.

Anyone who went trainspotting in the 50s and very early 60s will remember the pair from the Ian Allan locospotters guides, for their shape made them stand out from the rest.

In 1927, Sentinel built one of the locomotives, works number 7109 *Joyce*, and successfully trailed it at Newton Heath carriage works in Manchester.

The London Midland & Scottish railway was so impressed with the design that three production examples with slight modifications were ordered in 1929, and two were sent to the SDJR.

These two were required to haul coal trains below Radstock's Tyning Bridge, which had only a 10ft 10in clearance.

They were later renumbered by the LMS as 7190 and 7191 and following nationalisation became BR Nos 47190 and 47191. ➤

How low can you go? The 'Flying Bufferbeam' – reputed to be Britain's smallest standard gauge locomotive – looks like it was built for a breakdancing competition. It is seen in action in 1992. PHIL MARSH.

Pontyberem, the sole survivor of the Burry Port & Gweddreath Valley Railway, which used lower than normal locomotives and rolling stock to fit beneath former canal bridges. STUART THOMAS COLLECTION

Former Croydon gasworks Sentinel vertical-boilered locomotive *Joyce* at Midsomer Norton station being converted to represent one of its scrapped Somerset & Dorset sisters. ROBIN JONES

No 47191 was withdrawn in 1959 and the demolition of the bridge the following year rendered its sister locomotive redundant and it too was scrapped.

Yet *Joyce*, which spent its working life at Croydon gasworks, survived.

It eventually became part of a 56-locomotive static fleet owned by collector John Lees and kept at a private site in Shrewsbury.

The fleet was sold off early in 2002 and *Joyce* immediately came to the attention of revivalists who were attempting to recreate a section of the old Somerset & Dorset main line at Midsomer Norton station.

Their dream is to have an original S&D locomotive, but only two survive, 7F 2-8-0s, No 88 which is based on the West Somerset Railway and sister No 53809 which has its home at the Midland Railway-Butterley.

However, it was quickly realised that all that will be needed to convert *Joyce* into one of its 'successors' off the Shrewsbury production line is to lower and modify its cab. Apart from that, the locomotives are identical in every other respect.

Joyce has been repainted into BR black and it is hoped it will steam in 2010. Like *Alfred* and *Judy*, it will be offered for hire to other railways for special events as well as running on its 'home' line.

What happens when you get a standard gauge railway that has inherited several bridges that are too low?

That is the case at the Burry Port & Gwendeath Valley Railway near Llanelli, which was laid on the bed of the Kymer's Canal, the first canal in Wales, between 1865-69, when it was realised it could provide more efficient transport than an artificial waterway.

The canal bridges remained in situ, however, necessitating the use of both locomotives with low cabs and chimneys, and carriages and wagons which were lower than their counterparts on the rest of the national network.

The sole surviving Burry Port & Gwendreath Valley Railway steam locomotive is No 2 *Pontyberem*, supplied new by manufacturer Avonside in 1900. It ran on the line until 1914 after which it was sold in into industry, but in 1970 was bought for preservation by members of the Great Western Society at Didcot.

At one stage, seaside specials were run on the line to Burry Port, and comprised coal trucks cleaned out with temporary bench seats fitted – easily tackling the problem of carriages that might have been too high!

The railway authorities' concern over the worsening state of the track led to the line being rebuilt, with some of the sharp bends and steep gradients from the canal days

(inclined planes had been used on the waterway as well as lock gates) ironed out wherever possible. The line reopened to Pontyberem in August 1909 with the final eastern stretch to Cwm Mawr reopening on 29 January 1913.

The start of the new passenger service resulted in the purchase of second-hand carriages. Due to the tight loading gauge, those acquired could be loosely classified as former underground or commuter stock from various London railways.

The Metropolitan Railway had a surplus due to the ongoing electrification of services at that time. Other sources were the London & South Western Railway and the North London Railway.

The Great Western railway took over the line at the Grouping of 1922 and new locomotives were provide for the line along with some four-wheeled carriages. However, by 1939 their condition had deteriorated to the point where new 'low height' stock had to be specially built.

The line closed to passenger traffic on 21 September 1953, but it remained open for coal traffic. In 1965, British Railway reduced the height of the cabs of some Class 03 diesels hunters and sent them to work the line.

By 1983, most of these 03s were life expired and so cut-down Class 08 shunters replaced them.

Pontyberem and its train at Pontyberem c1909. STUART THOMAS COLLECTION

Judy and *Alfred* as Bill and Ben at the West Somerset Railway's Days Out with Thomas event in on 5 July 2009. The photographer's son Sean was fireman on *Alfred* that day.
ERIC BROOM

Pontyberem arrives at the Pontypool & Blaenavon Railway for restoration. GVRS

Operating on the 2ft 6in gauge Welshpool & Llanfair Light Railway is Barclay 0-4-0 tank engine *Douglas*, built in 1946 for the Provan gasworks system in Glasgow and roughly half the height of other steam engines on the line. It is seen working a full-size passenger train during the line's gala on 7 September 2009. FRED KERR

The line was finally closed in 1996 following the demise of the last open cast mines in the area. Most of the track on the final eight miles of main line is still in place but severely overgrown. Revivalists have looked at the line on several occasions. One group came up with the idea of converting the track to metre gauge and importing redundant Portuguese steam locomotives and carriages to work on it.

The Gwendraeth Railway Society is now working towards a revival. Its members have secured none other than *Potyberem* to work on it, moving it from the Great Western Society's base at Didcot Railway Centre to the Pontypool & Blaneavon Railway where it can be restored to running order.

The engine was modified during its time working for the National Coal Board and under the current restoration plans the locomotive will be restored as far as possible back to its appearance. The existing chimney and cab, both of which are life expired, will be replaced.

Also at Blaenavon is one of the cut-down 03s, No 03141, which is currently undergoing a full overhaul and is likely to be the Gwendraeth Railway Society's first operational engine. Incidentally, anyone wishing to help the society is invited to write to The Gwendraeth Railway Society, c/o Glanmorlais Uchaf, Llandyfaelog, Kidwelly Carmarthenshire SA17 5AP or email info@bpgv.co.uk

'At one stage, seaside specials were run on the line to Burry Port, and comprised coal trucks cleaned out with temporary bench seats fitted.'

In terms of preserved cut-down locomotives, I have been saving the best for last.

The Buckinghamshire Railway Centre at Quainton Road is home to the smallest standard gauge locomotive in Britain, which is so low that it is nicknamed 'the Flying Bufferbeam'.

Peckett No 1900 was built for Courtaulds Ltd's plant in Flint, North Wales in 1936 at a cost of £840. The plant was divided by the LMS Chester to Holyhead line, and the internal rail link between the two parts was through a very low tunnel through the main line embankment.

The locomotive's principal duty was shunting wagon loads of waste from the Rayon fibre manufacturing process onto the sea wall from where it was dumped.

The tunnel was in the dip of two very steep inclines and No 1900 had to work flat out down one side in order to gain sufficient momentum for the climb up the other, giving rise to safety fears.

Accordingly, in 1954, No 1900 was replaced by two engines, one on either side of the tunnel, the wagons being worked by a rope between the two.

The unique locomotive was not dumped but overhauled, given a new firebox and despatched to Courtaulds' Grimsby plant, where an extension was fitted to the cab and it was used work on factory construction trains. When the factory was built, Courtaulds obtained a Sentinel locomotive and No 1900 was kept as a spare.

The firm last used it in the early 60s and it then lay in store until it was bought for preservation and brought to Quainton in September 1971 for restoration.

For a time it was named *Jill*. During 1980 the engine returned to service and fitted with vacuum brakes, it was used on lightweight passenger trains – a first – and demonstration freight trains.

The locomotive spent the summer of 1983 working on the Lakeside & Haverthwaite Railway, also hauling some passenger trains.

At the time of writing, it is out of ticket and awaiting a heavy overhaul. ■

The seaside line that sparked a
transport revolution

To the untrained eye, Brighton's Volk's Electric Railway may appear to be just another seaside tramway, a relic from the resort's Victorian heyday. However, it is no less than Britain's first electric railway, and the oldest in the world to be still running, and therefore of paramount international importance.

Magnus Volk: pioneer of electricity, who even built an electric car in 1888.

Magnus Volk did not invent the electric railway. However, he brought the concept to Britain, and switched the country on.

The son of a German clockmaker, Magnus Volk was born at 35 (now 40) Western Road, Brighton, on 19 October 1851. Locally educated, he became apprenticed to a scientific instrument maker but on the death of his father in 1869 returned home to assist his mother run the family business. His real interest, however, lay in the worlds of science and engineering, in particular anything that worked on electricity.

In 1879, he successfully demonstrated the first telephone link in Brighton. The next year, he connected the first residential fire alarm to the fire station.

In 1880, he became the first resident of Brighton to fit electric lights to his house at 38 Dyke Road, and over the next four years went on to fit electric incandescent lighting

to the Royal Pavilion and its grounds, the Dome, the town museum, art gallery and library. Contacts made during this work proved instrumental in his most famous project of all.

On 4 August 1883, Volk unveiled a quarter-mile long 2ft gauge electric railway running from a site on the seashore opposite the town's aquarium to the Chain Pier. Power was provided by a 2hp Otto gas engine driving a Siemans D5 50-volt DC generator. A small electric car was fitted with a 1½hp motor giving a top speed of about 6mph.

Electric traction was by no means new. The first known electric locomotive was built by Scotsman, Robert Davidson of Aberdeen, in 1837 and was powered by galvanic cells. Davidson followed it up with a bigger locomotive named Galvani, which was exhibited at the Royal Scottish Society of Arts Exhibition in 1841.

Poster advertising the Brighton and Rottingdean Seaside Electric Railway as 'A Sea Voyage on Wheels'. NATIONAL RAILWAY MUSEUM

Car 7 begins its journey westwards from Aquarium station. CLEM RUTTER

A total of 160 passengers could be carried on the Brighton and Rottingdean Seaside Electric Railway's single car *Pioneer*, which was nicknamed 'Daddy Long Legs'. NATIONAL RAILWAY MUSEUM

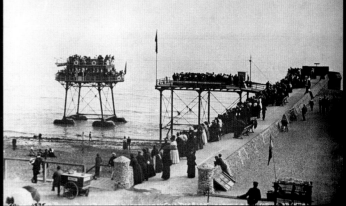

The Brighton terminus of the unique and short-lived sea railway. VERA

This second locomotive was tested on the Edinburgh & Glasgow Railway in September 1842, but the limited electric power available from batteries prevented its general use.

The world's first electric passenger train was demonstrated by Werner von Siemens in Berlin in 1879. It locomotive was driven by a 2.2 kW motor and the train which consisted of the locomotive and three cars reached a maximum speed of 13km/h, and over four months the train carried 90,000 passengers on a 320-yard circular track.

The electricity, provided by a nearby stationary dynamo, was supplied to the train through a third isolated rail situated between the tracks.

In 1881, the world's first electric tram line, also built by Siemens, opened in Lichterfelde, near Berlin, Germany.

The idea of an electric as opposed to steam locomotive may have originated in Scotland, but Volk brought it back to Britain in the form of a workable concept.

He soon sought powers to extend his westwards along the beach to the town boundary, but the council refused. Instead, he obtained permission to extend eastwards from the Aquarium to the Banjo Groyne and the Arch at Paston Place to provide workshop and power facilities. He also decided to widen the track to 2ft 8½in gauge, and he designed two more powerful and larger passenger cars.

The route followed the seashore, and needed timber trestles to bridge gaps in the shingle, and severe gradients down and up to allow the cars to pass under the town's Chain Pier.

The new line opened on 4 April 1884, at first using one car. The upgraded power plant in the Arch gave an output of 160 volts at 40 amps, more than enough to propel the two new cars along the 1400 yard-long railway. A loop complete with halt was provided halfway along the route for the cars to pass.

With the arrival of the second car, a five or six-minute service was provided daily, summer and winter, excepting Sundays, until 1903. The service operated until 1940 when the threat of invasion closed the railway during World War Two.

While local cab drivers and fishermen working from the beach were not impressed with the competition from the railway, it was a huge hit with the public. Two new cars, Nos 3 and 4, entered service in 1892, and a fifth car followed in 1897. In 1890, frustrated at his inability to extend beyond the Banjo Groyne to Rottingdean, it being blocked, Volks produced a scheme for a new kind of railway which ran through the sea itself.

The Brighton and Rottingdean Seashore Electric Railway consisted of two parallel 2ft 8½in gauge tracks, billed as 18ft gauge, the measurement between the outermost rails. The tracks were laid on concrete sleepers mortised into the bedrock.

The single car used on the railway was a 45ft by 22ft pier-like building which stood on four 23ft-long legs and weighed 45 tons. It was powered by electric motor.

It was officially named *Pioneer*, but many called it Daddy Long-Legs and the nickname stuck. Not only did it need a driver, but a qualified sea captain was on board at all times.

Uniquely in British railways again, the car was provided with lifeboats and other safety measures. Building of the second line began in 1894 and it officially opened on 28 November 1896, only to be severely damaged by a storm a week later. ➤

A Volk's Electric Railway two-car service running eastwards to Black Rock, as seen from the mound of shingle that hides Brighton's nudist beach. ROBIN JONES

Volk rebuilt the railway, including *Pioneer*, which had been turned onto its side, and it reopened in July 1897. The railway, arguably the most eccentric in Britain, also proved popular, but faced difficulties. High tide slowed the car down, and Volk did not have the finance to install more powerful motors.

In 1900, groynes built near the railway to prevent beach erosion were found to have led to underwater scouring under the sleepers and the line was closed for two months while repairs took place. The council decided to build a beach protection barrier, and told Volk to divert his line around it. He could not afford to do so, and so closed it

The track, car and other structures were sold for scrap, but some of the concrete sleepers can still be seen at low tide. A modern-day comparision might be made with the unique sea tractor at tidal Burgh

Island at Bigbury-on-Sea in south Devon, which takes passengers from the mainland to the island at high tide, on a platform carried on stilts.

After the Brighton & Rottingdean Seashore Electric Railway venture failed, Volk obtained permission to extend his first line beyond the Banjo Groyne to Black Rock and opened the extension in September 1901, bringing the total length of the railway to one-and-a-quarter miles.

The longer line needed more cars and three were added, and by 1926, the fleet had been brought up to 10. The last car built specifically for the railway was a winter car, which arrived in 1930.

In 1930, the redevelopment of Madeira Drive saw the railway cut back at the western end to a site opposite the aquarium. It was a setback for the line as the terminus was now no longer next to the pier entrance.

Sadly and short-sightedly, the line was also cut back by several hundred yards at the Black Rock end. The council decided to build a new swimming pool on the land currently occupied by the station and so cut the line even shorter.

The new Black Rock station was opened on 7 May 1937, when Volk, then 85, and the deputy mayor and Magnus Volk took joint control of Car 10 for a journey. It was Volk's last public appearance as he died peacefully at home13 days later. He is buried at St Wulfran's churchyard in Ovingdean near Brighton.

Control of the railway passed briefly to his son Herman. However, the 1938 Brighton Corporation (Transport) Act gave the local authority the powers to take over the railway.

At first the line was leased back to Herman, but on 1 April 1940 the corporation took full control, the last train running three months later before closure for the war years.

After hostilities ended, the council did much to upgrade the railway, replacing the rails and life-expired buildings. Services resumed on 15 May 1948, but winter services were suspended in 1954 and have been run only occasionally ever since. Original cars 1 and 2 were scrapped and replaced by two Southend Pier Railway trailer cars which, converted to motor cars became Nos 8 and 9 in the fleet.

During the late 60s and 70s, Brighton began to be severely hit by competition from cheap Mediterranean package holidays. The Black Rock swimming pool closed in 1978, leading to a further drop in passenger numbers on the railway.

Questions were asked as to whether the expense of keeping the railway open was justified, but in the end it was decided to keep the line open at least until its centenary in 1983. That event was a huge success, with Volk's youngest son Conrad driving a special train comprising cars 3 and 4. Afterwards, it was decided to keep the line open.

Services on the Volk's Electric Railway's elevated sections were often disrupted due to storm surges. The beach has since changed its profile and the shingle is now much higher, so the viaducts are not needed. ROBIN JONES COLLECTION.

Above: **Halfway station – is this Britain's smallest station building?** ROBIN JONES

Above right: **Two cars pass at Halfway station.** ROBIN JONES

Below: **The foundations of the Brighton and Rottingdean Seaside Electric Railway as seen at low tide.**

The successful launch of Volk's Electric Railway led to electric traction replacing steam as motive power on many railways, and today's electrified main lines can trace a lineage back to the little Brighton pioneer line. Here, a Eurostar unit speeds past Tallington on the East Coast Main Line. ROBIN JONES

Patronage is reasonably buoyant today, although there are many who have commented that it would be far greater if the line could in some way be re-extended westwards back to the pier entrance, and eastwards beyond Black Rock to the new Brighton marina.

As it is, first-time visitors who head straight from the main line railway station to the pier would not even guess that Volks Electric Railway exists. Does it provide public transport, or is it a Victorian anachronism limited to novelty value?

This writer believes that the heritage potential of the railway and surrounding attractions is huge. As stated earlier, Volks Electric Railway was not the first in the world to run on electricity, but all the earlier ones have long since passed into history. It was also the first in Britain. Therefore it should not be dismissed as a local antique, but a national attraction of immense historical importance.

By bringing it to Britain, Volk sowed seeds which may be deemed to have helped with the creation of the London underground and electrified overground suburban lines, the third-rail electric Southern Railway/Region and ultimately the inter-city trunk routes like the East and West Coast Main lines which form a backbone of the country's provincial transport system. In so many way it was a true 'first', and we should be shouting it from the rooftops. Secondly, the British seaside has seen a resurgence in recent years, with the popularity of holiday homes and then more people deciding not to go abroad because of poor exchange rates. Now is surely the time to capitalise.

The railway's western terminus, Aquarium station, stands opposite the Sealife Centre. However, this building is far more important than just another aquarium in a national chain. Dating from 1872, it is nothing less than the world's oldest working aquarium, conceived and designed by Eugenius Birch, the architect responsible for the West Pier, which is awaiting rebuilding after being left to decay and then gutted by fire. The interior of the aquarium has been kitted out to look like something from a Jules Verne submarine theme park, and its ambience dovetails so well with the early electric railway that runs outside.

While Brighton is famous for the Royal Pavilion, there are enough classic Victorian and Edwardian 'seaside' structures and features that could be enhanced to offer a package by which the town could be sold to visitors from both home and overseas who wish to revel in the finer delights of yesteryear, with the railway at its core.

At the time of writing, there is no immediate threat to close the railway, but it clearly could offer so much more. Since 1995, it has been supported by a growing band of enthusiasts under the banner of the Volk's Electric Railway Association, who, on occasions, even take over the running of the trains.

If you fancy doing something a little more elaborate than bucket and spading at Brighton, contact the group via membership secretary Alan James, 13 Rudyard Road, Woodingdean, Brighton BN2 6UB, or on alanjames812@hotmail.com

Magnus Volk has also been immortalised in Brighton's own Walk of Fame, the brainchild of local resident David Courtney, the man who discovered pop star Leo Sayer back in the 70s. Based on the Hollywood Walk of Fame, it is the only one of its kind in Britain. All the 100 names are laid in a liner alongside the resort's waterfront development, and Volk is up there with the likes of Dame Anna Neagle, Ruyard Kipling and Chris Eubank.

In terms of the impact that electric railways had on British transport, maybe he is the greatest Brightonian of them all. ∎

Seeing double:
the steam camels

We have all heard of the phrase 'iron horse'. As we have seen, Beamish Museum has recreated a Steam Elephant. And yes, there was also a steam camel...

French engineer Charles Lartigue wanted to become another Richard Trevithick or George Stephenson, either devising a completed new form of transport or making vast improvements on one that already existed.

Maybe he left it too late, or perhaps he thought too long and hard about it. Perhaps he found a solution to a problem that did not really exist. Or in solving one problem he created two...

Lartigue was born in Toulouse in 1834, the year of Trevithick's death.

Sometime in his forties, he visited Algeria and saw camels, the 'ship of the desert', carrying heavy loads balanced in panniers on their backs.

The sight provided a flash of inspiration to devise an all-new type of railway.

Instead of locomotives and stock running on two rails fixed to the ground, why not have a single rail at waist height but carried on A-shaped trestles?

The locomotives, carriages and wagons would then sit astride the track just like the camels' panniers.

By 1881, Lartigue had a 56-mile A-shaped monorail running across the Algerian desert.

Its principal purpose was to transport esparto grass, with mules pulling trains of panniers carried by the trestle-mounted rail.

It was a case of a genuine innovation, as while the shifting sands of the desert would have made a conventional rail line virtually unusable, the single raised rail was a distinct advantage.

For Lartigue was a case of first Algeria, then the world... whether or not it had sufficient deserts.

In 1886, he displayed a sample length of his line to an exhibition in London in a bid to convince others it was a superior system. By then, of course, Brunel's broad gauge had but a few years left, and Stephenson's 4ft 8½in standard gauge was the norm.

At the same time, the folk of North Kerry in Ireland were pressing for the railway network to be expanded, bringing all of its benefits to the more remote communities... such as Listowel and Ballybunion.

Their demands reached a minister's desk in Westminster... and somewhere along the line, it was decided to test Lartigue's innovative idea by building a nine-mile line between the two towns.

One of the original locomotives in Ballybunion station.

The replica Listowel & Ballybunion locomotive at one of the points, or 'switches'.

The Listowel & Ballybunion Railway was opened on 1 March 1888 at a cost of £30,000. It is the town's claim to global fame as the site of the world's first steam monorailway.

Yet it was not a true monorail in the strictest sense of the word, for on either side of the trestle was another rail, on which unpowered stabilising wheels fitted to all the engines and wagons stopped them from overbalancing.

The famous Leeds firm of locomotive builders, Hunslet, supplied three engines to the line, designed by no less a person than Anatole Mallet. Nos 1 and 2 left the Hunslet works on 10 October 1887, and No 3 followed a week later.

They were 0-6-0s – or rather, 0-3-0s. Looking like steam Siamese twins, they were specially built with two boilers in order to balance on the track, and accordingly two fireboxes, one of which had to be stoked by the driver.

They also had powered tenders for auxiliary use on hills. The tender wheels were driven by two cylinders via spur gears. Two small chimneys were fitted to each tender to discharge the exhaust steam from these cylinders. ➤

Passengers crossing the rails on a steps bogie.

The tenders had two double-flanged wheels which could also be driven by a geared auxiliary engine for dealing with heavy loads on gradients; when in use it was engaged by a friction clutch, so the machinery would not be driven uselessly in normal operation. Therefore, the Listowel & Ballybunion engines could be said to have a wheel configuration of 0-3-0 + 0-2-0, all but unique in the history of locomotive engineering. However, the boilers were unable to generate enough steam to run the auxiliary engine, and it was never used.

The trains carried freight, cattle, sand from the beaches (not the local desert, as there wasn't one) and passengers, who included Ballybunion schoolchildren being carried to Listowel's secondary schools, Kerry and Limerick residents heading for the beach resort of Ballybunion and golfers travelling to the fledgling golf course at Ballybunion, which was to develop into one of the best in the world.

Freight loads had to be evenly balanced. If a farmer wanted to send a cow to market, he would have to send two calves to balance it. They would travel back on opposite sides of the same freight wagon, thereby balancing each other.

Likewise, passengers could not pass from one side of a carriage to another while in motion. A footbridge was built into one end of some of the passenger coaches, allowing them to cross from one side of the line to the other while the train was stopped at a station.

A major problem with the trestle track was that it was impossible to build level crossings.

When the track met a road, a double-sided drawbridge had to be constructed, and an attendant was required to operate it.

Where farmers' tracks crossed the line, level crossings based on the principle of a turntable were provided. These were locked before and after use, and the farmer provided with a key.

Once unlocked, the track could be swivelled to one side to allow the crossing to be used.

Both the swivelling and drawbridge type crossings were automatically linked to signals which stopped any approaching trains, and road traffic was always given priority.

Conventional railway points could not be used, so to access sidings and passing loops, a large number of turntables was needed.

A late Victorian drawing of the Lartigue trestleway system.

What a much earlier innovator like Brunel would have made of Lartigue's system when he drew up plans for his Great Western Railway in 1836, nobody will ever know. Had there been a Dragon's Den back then, the words 'I'm out' might just about have cropped up more than once at this stage in the proceedings.

Like so many lines serving rural lines, the Listowel & Ballybunion just about broke even throughout its life. What is remarkable, however, is that life lasted 36 years.

The 10 January 1920 issue of *The New Illustrated* magazine contained an article titled An Unknown British Railway By S T James.

He writes: 'There are in this world of ours a remarkably high number of freakish transport concerns labelled as 'railways' and one of the most peculiar of them is the Listowel & Ballybunion line, in the county of Kerry, Ireland.

'This railway was built in 1888 for the special purpose of developing Ballybunion (Lord Kitchener's birthplace) as a seaside resort. It took only six months to build, is nine and a half miles long, and cost £3000 per mile, an extremely low figure, as many other British railway companies could testify'.

Instead of a gleaming metal track, the permanent way consists of light A-shaped trestles, about three and a half feet high, and placed across the ground at about the same

distance one from another. The object of a permanent way of this description is to obviate the heavy expense of levelling the ground. By slightly varying the lengths of the trestles, the line can run fairly evenly over the grass, up hill and down dale'.

He continued: 'There are three locomotives, but only one is used at a time. The two most efficient ones work a week each in turn, while the third is kept In reserve for special occasions.

'Naturally, having to run on a single elevated line of rail, the engines have to be so constructed that they will balance, or, to use naval language, maintain an even keel. This is ensured by making each locomotive with two boilers, two funnels, two tenders, two smokeboxes, stacks etc. In fact, a Listowel & Ballybunion locomotive is just like two ordinary ones joined together in the middle.

'It is claimed that these engines can haul a load of 240 tons over the trestleway at 30mph.

'The passenger coaches and goods wagons are, of course, built on similar lines, each consisting of a double interior, and as it is necessary to have some connection between each half of the passenger vehicles, a stairway is provided via which travellers can pass from one side to the other, over the top of the coach.

'Altogether, there are 11 passenger coaches, providing seating accommodation for 52 first-class and 228 third-class passengers.

Hunslet makers' photograph of an original Listowel & Ballybunion locomotive.

There are also 17 sand wagons and five goods wagons, with two brake vans. Truly an imposing array of rolling stock.

'Perhaps the most amusing thing of all to English visitors is the shunting. The various sidings on which vehicles are to be arranged, or 'marshalled', are all disconnected from the main line, and before a vehicle can be pushed on or drawn off such a siding, a portion of trestle way must be swung into position to connect the two.

'Imagine, then, the nature of each shunting operation. A wagon has been placed on line No 1. The next vehicle is for line No 3. So the trestle track has to be unbolted from the ground, disconnected with line No 1, moved into a position that will connect it with line No 3, connected up, bolted down, and then – well, there we are! How very different to our method of merely pulling over a lever to alter the points.

'Connecting with the Ballybunion terminus of the line is a short branch of half a mile whereon sand wagons are loaded. This branch line is cleared once a day, and since it runs along the main road, the trestle track can only be allowed to remain fixed in a position during the hour or so when the train is running along it. After that it is uprooted and left lying along the roadside for the rest of the day.

'Just before the train comes along on the morrow, a railway official will arrive to reconstruct the permanent way. ➤

A hand-coloured postcard view of the Listowel & Ballybunion Railway in 1900.

THE HUNSLET ENGINE CO. LTD *Engineers* LEEDS ENGLAND

0-6-0 TYPE
SINGLE RAIL TENDER ENGINE

Manufacturer's advertisement for the Lartigue locomotive. There were no customers apart from the Listowel & Ballybunion.

'A ride over the Listowel & Ballybunion Railway is an experience not likely to be forgotten. As the time for departure draws near, the loading of the passengers has to be adjusted in order that the train shall balance evenly. The weight of travellers in the left half must be approximately equal to the weight of those in the right half.

'Guard and stationmaster jointly arrange the balancing, walking each down one side and calling to the other the number in each half of the coach. If perchance there should be 20 in one half and only 12 on the other, four of the 20 have to leave and proceed via the portable bridge to the other side of the train.

'Local residents assert that one day there arrived at the station just before the train started two engaged couples, a very fat pair and a very lean pair. The first-class carriages, for which these people held tickets, only hold two on each side, and the two fat ones climbed in one half, while the two thin ones sat in the other. This, of course, quite upset the balance of the train, and eventually someone – it needed an Irishman, too – intimated to the devoted lovers that they must part company. So a fat male and a thin female exchanged places, and so well did the alteration suit, that when the train reached its destination the change of partners had been made permanent.

'There are no stations such as we are accustomed to, but a marked-out piece of land serves. The general manager's office is about the size of an ordinary platelayer's cabin, and this official undertakes every administrative duty connected with the line, being passenger, goods, and locomotive manager, permanent-way inspector and Lord High Admiral of everything'.

The downfall of the line came not because of greater competition from motor transport, which killed off many British light railways in the 20s and 30s, but through damage caused during the Irish Civil War from 1921-23.

The line closed in 1924 and everything was scrapped except a short section of the track.

It seemed that the Listowel & Ballybunion would remain immortalised as the definitive oddball line which cropped up in any book covering narrow gauge railways of Britain.

A static replica of one of the French monorail locomotives in Panissières.

The year 1988 saw the centenary of the opening of the monorail and local politician and Lartigue enthusiast Michael Guerin produced a history of the line.

Michael Barry of Lisselton had already assembled 50 metres of salvaged track and an original carriage and Michael Foster had written a valuable book on the Lartigue. There were many locals who, buoyed by the success of railway revival schemes elsewhere, became determined to restore their piece of technological eccentricity.

A movement to restore part of the line offering passenger rides developed from small beginnings, and in the mid-90s the Lartigue Restoration Committee was set up with Jack McKenna, who had travelled on the footplate of the original line as its president.

Alan Keef Ltd, an accomplished narrow-gauge locomotive builder based in Ross-on-Wye, Herefordshire, was contracted by the Lartigue Monorailway Restoration Committee, a voluntary organisation from Listowel, to build a replica locomotive, but for reasons of economy (one boiler is expensive enough to maintain and overhaul,

let alone two) and ease of operation, while it resembled one of the original steam engines, it was powered by a diesel motor.

Keef was also contracted to supply two third-class carriages. No drawings for the original carriages survived, so the firm closely modelled the new coaches on them as far as possible, using photographs and the memory of surviving passengers.

After much work and fundraising by the committee, work started on the building of the new line on a site on John B Keane Road in Listowel in November 2000.

In 2003, a 1000-metre section of Lartigue monorail on the trackbed of the former North Kerry line was opened, wih three points, two turntables and three platforms representing Listowel, Lisselton and Ballybunion.

The ride on the modern-day monorail starts less than 100 metres from the point where the original began its journey to Ballybunion. The site of the original Lartigue Listowel Terminal is preserved in a park adjacent to the new monorail, along with the bases of two points and the foundations of the engine house.

So today it is possible to ride on what must surely be a candidate for the title of the weirdest railway in the British Isles.

However, Listowel & Ballybunion was not unique.

In the wake of the opening of the Irish line, longstanding demands by up to 5000 residents of Panissières in the Loire region for a 'modern' transport link to Feurs and the national rail network were met by the building of a 10-mile Lartigue monorail in the 1890.

The route passed through Donzy, Cottance and Salvizinet, and had five stations, but no level crossings. A pair of locomotives, named Feurs and Panissières, were built by Bietrix of Saint-Etienne, a firm which specialised in manufacturing mining equipment. There were five carriages, each seating 26 passengers.

Testing of the completed line in August 1895 was less than satisfactory. A VIP trip

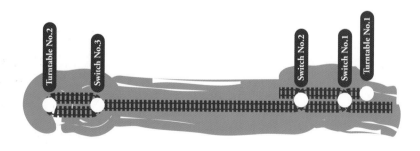

The replica Lartigue train in Platform 1. The train leaves Platform 1, travels via Switch No 1 through Platform 2 and down the main line for about 500 metres, then through Switch No 3 to Platform 3 where the train stops and the passengers alight. The train travels at about 15mph while on the main line, approximately the same speed as the original trains.

carrying the Prefect of the Loire was run on 14 August 1896 from Feurs to Panissières, but the train broke down after the locomotive failed to produce enough steam. The locomotives also failed regularly to tackle the gradients of 2.5 per cent with curves as tight as 25-metre radius.

After the local council agreed to subsidise the bringing of the monorail up to scratch, permission to operate it was finally given by the powers that be. However, the company then said that it no longer had the resources to operate the line, which was duly sold to a scrap merchant in Lyon in 1902.

What is believed to have been the last Lartigue monorail to be built was opened in the Mojave Desert, California, by the Sierra Salt Corporation, in the mid-20s. It carried magnesium salts from the company's mine in the Crystal Hills to the railhead at Trona.

Unlike the French example, it worked, but lasted only two years before modern developments in magnesium extraction made the mine redundant.

Lartigue had died in 1907, and there were no further takers for his steam camels.

*Pictures supplied by Paddy Keane, volunteer on the Lartigue Monorailway. ∎

'So today it is possible to ride on what must surely be a candidate for the title of the weirdest railway in the British Isles.'

A Lartigue train leaving Listowel station.

Original Lartigue train arriving at Ballybunion.

One of 17 'flying drawbridge' crossings on the Listowel & Ballybunion.

Go to jail!

Seaside miniature railways were for decades standard fare for the traditional British holiday, with every sizeable bucket and spade resort having at least one, and generations of happy campers holding fond memories of them. Billy Butlin even bought redundant full-size steam engines for display at his camps when they were no longer wanted by British Railway. However, in one far-flung and very desolate corner of the coast, seaside railways meant not holidays, but hell!

It was in 1935 that a group of 32 boys set off on a marathon trek from Stafford to the coast of Lincolnshire.

Under the supervision of three adults, they walked all 100 miles, stopping in village halls overnight.

And when they reached their destination, a bleak and deserted expanse of farmland overlooking salt marshes where the River Witham meets The Wash near Boston, they erected tents as accommodation.

It sounds every bit like some great Boy Scout jamboree of which Lord Baden-Powell would have been justifiably proud.

Far from it. The boys were all young offenders and the adults who accompanied them were prison officers.

And the trip was not organised by the scouting movement but the Borstal institution authorities, with the sole purpose of having the boys build their own detention centre.

Not only that, but once brick-built accommodation replaced the tents, they would be given purposeful work on the surrounding fenland.

In the days of the 'Grow For Britain' campaign, this new Borstal would run its own

farm, but in doing so, 600 acres of salt marsh would have to be reclaimed from the sea, continuing a trend that had begun around the muddy shores of The Wash in Roman times.

That posed few logistics problems; a ready supply of free manpower, or rather boypower, was immediately available, and they were allocated the task of building a new sea wall and a set of dykes to hold the tides back.

In doing so, the boys would complete a task already begun by nature – the destruction of Lincolnshire's first seaside resort, Freiston Shore.

Here lies a classic example of a 'lost' resort, where the waves that once raced over its sandy beach now break over mudflats more than half a mile to the east, and what remains of the visitor facilities are now high and dry.

More than 200 years ago, Freiston Shore boasted a fine stretch of sandy beach. In the middle of the 18th century, when Skegness was still a small fishing village, visitors arrived in droves to Freiston Shore to bathe and drink the seawater for medicinal purposes.

For the Victorians, Freiston Shore was a popular year-round resort. Horse races were held on the shore between Freiston and Butterwick and proved enormously popular.

Working on the train gang: the daily life of young offenders at North Sea Camp in the 1950s.

Spoil from salt marshes tipped to build up the sea wall at Freiston Shore, in a picture dating from the early 1970s.

Britain's only prison railway was used to build colossal sea defences by hand.

However, The Wash has been slowly silting up since prehistoric times, long before bad King John lost his treasure in its quicksands, and the muddy sediment suspended in the waves from the discharge of rivers slowly built up on the beach, encouraging the formation of mudflats. Also, the opening of the Witham Cut by the Boston port authorities further widened the area of salt marshes between Freiston and the sea.

Eventually, Freiston Shore found itself cut off from the sea, and while the Great Northern Railway line to 'Skeggy' was opened in 1873, Freiston was never connected to the national network. So visitors turned overnight to the more accessible destination which had its sandy beach intact.

Not to be outdone, Freiston Shore managed to retain some of its former popularity. The salt marshes which covered the once-golden sands became a popular haunt for shooting and fishing, with visitors from the Midlands and Yorkshire arriving to stop in the two hotels, the Plummers and the Marina. Stalls were set up on the sea wall and buses ferried in trippers from Boston.

But as the salt marshes took over more and more of the beach, the hotels became non-viable. The bigger of the two, the 23-bedroom Marina, closed down – part of it stands as a run alongside the original sea wall today – while the Plummers became a pub and was eventually split into six units and sold off as private accommodation.

Largely forgotten, yes, but Freiston Shore was to be given a railway after all.

Building the huge land reclamation dykes called for a means of transporting huge amounts of earth around – and what better than tipper trucks on rails.

A 2ft gauge tramway system was introduced, whereby lengths of portable track were laid in place along the construction sites, and the Borstal boys pushed the tipper wagons along it by hand.

The railway system soon spread out over the marshes and reclaimed fens, with a 'main line' running for three miles from North Sea Camp – so named because it started out as exactly that, a tented campsite – to Freiston Shore below the original sea wall.

Generations of young miscreants aided Mother Nature in pushing the sea wall further back. In time the railway switched from manpower to modern traction, in the form of Lister four-wheeled diesel locomotives, a move greatly welcomed by the exhausted inmates.

A network of sidings served the various workshops and maintenance depots at the prison camp itself. ➤

Britain's only prison railway was like a giant train set, with portable lengths of track laid across dykes to aid salt marsh reclamation by the inmates.

Horse racing along the sands at Freiston Shore in the early 19th century. The sands had long since vanished by the time Borstal boys began reclaiming saltmarsh.

This jailbird has flown: a nest was found growing inside the engine compartment of one of the railway's diesels.

Tory peer Jeffrey Archer, who was an inmate at North Sea Camp while he was serving four years for perjury.

From there, the line headed northwards, with branches diverging at various points to reclamation sites, where temporary track would be laid.

A few hundred yards from Freiston Shore stood the 'dining room'. This was/is a Nissen-type hut where locomotives and stock were stored, and prisoners working on the reclamation schemes were served hot meals at lunchtime to save them having to trudge all the way back to the camp.

The stock mainly comprised hand-operated tipper wagons, while some chassis had been modified to carrying winches and water pumps.

The railway remained in use until the 1970s as more and more salt marsh was reclaimed by the boys.

The term Borstal went out of use (it took its name from the quite innocent Kent village where the first such establishment was tried as an experiment), and the young offenders institution became an adult prison in 1988.

By that time the railway had fallen into disuse, (in its latter years, much of the manpower used in hauling large amounts of spoil and mud from the coast had been replaced by a dragline) and it was eventually decided that no more land could be reclaimed from the sea. The Wash had reached the equilibrium position where further deposited sediment was being just as quickly removed by the currents, and any eastward extension of the defences might prove impossible to maintain in the face of freak tides. In more recent times, some of the reclaimed land at Freiston Shore has been 'given back' to The Wash as part of a modern sea defence policy of 'managed retreat'.

The fleet of six diesel locomotives was placed into store, the temporary track piled high next to the old sea wall beyond the Plummers Hotel where some tipper wagons were also left to rot on a siding, and the main line became overgrown and, level crossings apart, covered by a thick layer of turf.

Is this what you call a branch railway line, or it is a trunk route?

These carriages were built by prisoners under an abortive revival scheme.

One of the prison line's Lister diesel locomotives as new.

HM Prison North Sea Camp displays one of its railway's diesel locomotive and a rake of tipper wagons at its main entrance.

'A 2ft gauge tramway system was introduced, whereby lengths of portable track were laid in place along the construction sites, and the Borstal boys pushed the tipper wagons along it by hand.'

One of the locomotives, Lister No 33651 of 1949, and three wagons were taken for preservation at HM Prison College at Newbold Revel near Rugby, where they were placed on open display.

Believed to be Britain's only internal prison railway, the potential of the railway was not lost on one of the previous governors, who in the 1980s hatched a revival plan.

He had a series of carriages built on the four-wheel wagon chassis from redundant tipper wagons, and inmates in the carpentry shop built a series of 'station buildings' which were to be erected along the line.

Sadly, this venture fizzled out, and the plywood-bodied carriages remain locked in the 'dining hut'.

A subsequent governor appointed in 2002 hatched more grandiose plans, and planned to fully revive the railway, opening it to the public on high days and holidays. He went as far as to appoint a full-time project director with railway preservation experience for the purpose and

hoped to open a café at Freiston Shore so that refreshments could be served to birdwatchers.

Sadly, the scheme came to grief, after he parted company with the prison service.

The authorities then took a decision to get rid of the railway once and for all, and sold it off piece by piece at auction in March 2005.

The auction was handled by Sleaford estate agents Pygott & Crone, and bidding was brisk, despite the fact that the little railway had been rusting away for three decades and was mostly overgrown.

Some of the wagons had been left in situ since the railway was last used, and had tree trunks growing through them. And when inspected, one of the locomotives had a bird's nest in the engine compartment.

Unlike the prison's inmates, which famously included the disgraced Tory peer and novelist Jeffrey Archer after he received a four-year stint for perjury, railway enthusiasts from all over Britain queued up to visit the camp for the sale.

The Cleethorpes Coast Light Railway, spent £650 on buying spare locomotive parts.

Herefordshire locomotive builder Alan Keef bought half a mile of track for a bargain £400 – but will now have to send workers nearly 200 miles to lift it.

Another enthusiast forked out £2200 for nine huge heaps of rusting portable track sections which had been lying in a field at Freiston Shore waiting in vain for the Borstal boys to return.

One of the locomotives sold for £2576, while the same buyer acquired the chassis of another for £1600.

Perhaps the best bargain of all was the £60 paid by the private North Ings Farm Railway Museum at Dorrington, near Ruskington. For his money, the owner picked up a fleet of six carriages – made out of plywood by prisoners and fitted to wagon chassis during a previous attempt to revive the railway.

The money would scarcely have bought him three Hornby OO scale model coaches! ∎

The Docker's Umbrella

While London and other world cities burrowed underground to create railways to bypass surface traffic congestion, Liverpool went in the opposite direction – and built the world's first elevated electric railway.

Gladstone Dock station as seen from ground level with Set No 41 entering.
COLOUR-RAIL

The Liverpool Overhead Railway can claim another global first for British railway engineering.
It was the world's first electrically operated overhead railway, and also the first to be protected by electric automatic signals.

Opening in 1893 and closing in 1956, the elevated line provided quick and effective transport for generations of Merseyside dock workers, and there are many who believe it went before its time.

At a time when steam reigned supreme, and electric traction was still the domain of early inventors such as Magnus Volk, the Liverpool Overhead Railway Company was formed in 1888, although a railway along the route – linking Liverpool's docks – had been mooted as early as 1852.

By the 1880s, the city's dock network was virtually complete, but the offshoot of it was major traffic congestion in Dock Road – and that was before the invention of the motor car.

The problem was exacerbated by the many railway level crossings which connected goods stations and dockside lines. As trade boomed it was obvious that passenger traffic had to be accommodated away from the cargo routes.

A prominent group of businessmen formed the Liverpool Overhead Railway Company and obtained powers to build the line.

Engineers Sir Douglas Fox and James Henry Greathead opted for electric traction to eradicate the possibility of sparks from the burning coal of steam locomotives setting fire to flammable cargo nearby.

Building started in 1889 and the line, nicknamed the 'Docker's Umbrella' because it ran above ground, was opened on 4 February 1893, by the Marquis of Salisbury.

Built to standard gauge, it ran six miles from Alexandra Dock to Herculaneum Dock, with 11 intermediate stations along

A scene on the line in the 30s. LIVERPOOL MUSEUMS

the line, at Brocklebank, Canada, Sandon, Clarence, Princes, Pier Head, James Street, Canning, Wapping, Brunswick and Toxteth. It was predominantly carried on iron viaducts, with a corrugated iron decking, onto which the tracks were laid.

The company quickly realised that passenger ticket sales outside working hours were poor and decided to extend the line to tap in residential areas. Accordingly, the railway was extended northwards to Seaforth Sands on 30 April 1894 and southwards to Dingle on 21 December 1896. Dingle was the railway's only underground station and was located on Park Road. The southern extension from Herculaneum Dock involved a 200ft lattice girder bridge spanning the Cheshire Lines goods yard and boring a half-mile tunnel through the sandstone cliff to Park Road.

Passengers were bemused; if they were catching an overhead train, why should they have to descend steps to a subway leading to an underground station?

The final extension was northwards, linking the railway to the Lancashire & Yorkshire Railway's North Mersey Branch on 2 July 1905.

The L&Y ran some of its own specially built vehicles on the line on occasions such as race meetings at Aintree. The overhead suffered extensive damage from Luftwaffe bombs during World War Two, but it was quickly repaired to maintain the smooth operation of the docks.

Unusually, because it was very much a local affair, it was not nationalised with the rest of Britain's railways by the Labour government in 1948.

After the war, the Liverpool Overhead Railway Company began to modernise its carriages, fitting sliding doors in some of its 19 units.

The line continued to carry large volumes of passengers, especially dockers, and was an integral part of the city's transport system.

However, the iron curved deck plates which carried the railway were prone to corrosion in the sea air – and this was compounded by exhaust from steam locomotives on the docks railway which ran below. ➤

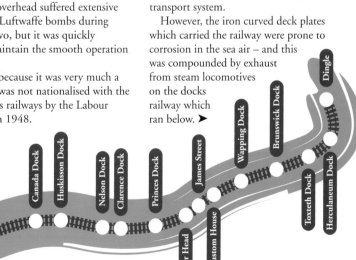

Remedial work estimated at £4-million was way outside the resources of the railway company, which looked in vain to both Liverpool City Council and the Mersey Docks and Harbour Board for financial assistance.

When no bailout was forthcoming, the company went into voluntary liquidation and closed on 30 December 1956, despite protests from passengers.

The final trains each left either end of the line, marking the closure with a loud bang as they passed each other. Both trains were full to capacity with supporters and company staff.

The railway was replaced by Liverpool Corporation bus service route No 1, which was by no means as fast as the overhead line, because of traffic congestion. Repeated public calls for the railway to reopen went unheeded by local authorities.

Demolition of the elevated railway and its sale for scrap began in September 1957 and took a year.

All that remained were upright columns in the walls at Wapping, the tunnel portal at Dingle and Dingle station, which became used as a garage. Liverpool's transport world first therefore passed into history overnight, but is still remembered with much fondness.

Above: A surviving Liverpool Overhead Railway car in the possessions of the city's museum's service. LIVERPOOL MUSEUMS

Left: A plaque marking the location of the overhead railway. LIVERPOOL MUSEUMS

Below: Going up in the world: a refurbished Liverpool Overhead Railway set crosses the main road at Pier Head. COLOUR-RAIL

Set No 20 enters James Street station.
COLOUR-RAIL

Its fame would soon, however, be eclipsed by another great Merseyside product, for while it was being demolished, a local teenage rock and roll group called the Quarrymen, inspired by blues music from the United States imported via the docks, were giving performances in the city. Four years later, they became the Beatles.

If you want to glimpse this unusual yet groundbreaking railway, it is featured in the 1951 film *The Clouded Yellow*, and in *Of Time and the City*, a 'cinematic autobiographical poem' produced by British film-maker Terence Davies to celebrate Liverpool's 2008 reign as Capital of Culture.

Furthermore, in 2010/11, part of the line will be 'reborn' as an exhibit inthe new £72-million Museum of Liverpool. The biggest newly built national museum in Britain for over a century, it is also the world's first national museum devoted to the history of a regional city, reflecting Liverpool's global significance through its unique geography, history and culture.

The exhibit will stand 16ft above the ground just like the original.

A surviving overhead railway 40ft third class carriage taken from the museum's storeroom at Bootle will be installed.

The exhibit will allow visitors to walk underneath, giving the same view of the line as the dockers had.

Admission to the museum will be free. ■

Above: **A computer-generated impression of the Port City gallery at the new Museum of Liverpool with the overhead railway carriage in place.** LIVERPOOL MUSEUMS

Right: **Remains of an upright at Wapping Dock.** ROBIN JONES

Below: **The railway as seen in the 1920s.** LIVERPOOL MUSEUMS

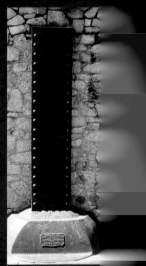

The entire steam fleet lines up outside the shed at New Romney. RHDR

The railway town of Romney Marsh

The Romney Hythe & Dymchurch Railway has long claimed to be the world's smallest public railway, its 15in gauge locomotives and stock running on a 'main line in miniature'. It runs for 13½ miles from Hythe to Dungeness, which has over the past century become a unique railway 'town' by the back door at Britain's south-easternmost corner.

Dungeness has that distinctive 'end of the world' feeling. The name is Old Norse for 'headland' and that is exactly what it is – Kent's version of Land's End or John O'Groats jutting out into the English Channel at the extremity of south-east England.

Headlands are normally associated with cliffs, but windblown isolated Dungeness comprises shingle – and lots of it. In fact, it is one of the biggest expanses of shingle in the world, and its rich flora and fauna – there are over 600 different types of plant and many rare insects such as moths, bees and beetles, and spiders found nowhere else in Britain – have seen it declared a Site of Special Scientific interest. Inadvertently, it has also become

a place of great railway interest too, without even trying.

It is no Crewe, Derby, Swindon or Eastleigh, but that has not stopped Dungeness from developing as a railway 'town'. Perhaps 'town' is the wrong word, for Dungeness is a settlement scattered at random with houses plonked all over the shingle, with no fenced-off gardens and linked only by telegraph poles and wires – a real 'wild west' outback scenario.

Many of these houses began life as Victorian railway carriages, the bodies sold off as homes for Dungeness fishermen when they were withdrawn from service.

The Southern Railway owned much of the land around Dungeness, and the coaches

would be brought there by rail in the 1920s, down the branch line from Appledore.

That line was opened by the Lydd Railway Company on 7 December 1881, being worked from 16 February 1882 by the South Eastern Railway. The company extended the line by building a branch from Lydd to New Romney which opened on 19 June 1884. In January 1895 the Lydd Railway Company was taken over by the South Eastern which became part of the South Eastern & Chatham Railway three years later.

More railway bungalow cottages followed over the years. Some were moved there in the 1950s to house workers when the nearby Dungeness nuclear power station was built. They were intended to be only temporary accommodation, but ended up being lived in ever since.

For those who could afford no better, the carriages formed cheap and instant accommodation. Starting out as basic coach bodies minus the chassis, the occupants extended and improved them, boxing in the roofs and then added chimneys and fireplaces at the rear, followed by extensions. ➤

Two Pacifics a size apart: *Flying Scotsman*, which went on to become the world's most famous railway locomotive, lines up against the Romney, Hythe & Dymchurch Railway's No 7 *Typhoon* at King's Cross depot in the mid-20s. ROBIN JONES COLLECTION

Opposite page: Davey Paxman 4-8-2 No 6 *Samson* arrives with a train at Dungeness, with the flat shingle wastes stretching as far as the eye can see. This photograph is taken from Dungeness Old Lighthouse, one of five to be built on the headland, and which is open to visitors prepared to climb its 169 steps. DAVID STAINES

Opposite the Britannia pub stands a white bungalow, the shape of the tongue and groove panelling which covers it just about betrays its origins as a railway coach. It was once a royal saloon for no less than Queen Victoria. Most other coach bodies at Dungeness are much less aristocratic.

Over the years, as more city folk 'discovered' Dungeness, the carriage houses became trendy and highly sought after as weekend retreats.

Not only that, but they came to the eye of architects and designers who stepped in to convert them into stylish and futuristic luxury dwellings – but with the original carriage still inside.

Standing in the shadow of Dungeness spower station area is a row of carriage homes, and what to the untrained eye seems to be an all-new modern wooden bungalow dwelling with glass front and veranda. From an angle, you can see the reflection of a railway carriage in the window. That is

Surveying the scene: Captain Howey (left) and Henry Greenly (right) on the site of New Romney station in 1925. DEREK SMITH COLLECTION

exactly what it is: the carriage now forms a state-of-the-art modern kitchen room inside the 'new' dwelling.

These carriages may have been cheap to buy when first offloaded by the railway – some cost as little as £10 – but recent asking prices have placed many well upwards of £200,000.

The railway that brought the coaches to Dungeness closed to passengers on 6 March 1967. The terminus, New Romney & Littlestone-on-Sea, was closed and the rails cut back as far as Dungeness, where a loading point for nuclear fuel for the A and B power stations was created. That line still exists today, and there have been calls to reopen it for passengers to Lydd-on-Sea airport.

As we have seen, while we may have a notion of what constitutes a 'normal' railway, the concept has a multitude of applications. A primary example of an 'unusual' manifestation of the railway principle can be seen at Dungeness, where a series of ramshackle narrow-gauge tracks have been laid from the coastal road to the high shingle ridge overlooking the sea.

Laurel and Hardy were the VIP guests at the reopening of the line to Dungeness in 1947. ROBIN JONES COLLECTION

Typhoon being turned at Hythe in late evening. RHDR

This bungalow is said to include a royal saloon used by Queen Victoria. ROBIN JONES

Another railway carriage bungalow, with the Old Lighthouse behind it. ROBIN JONES

These 'Heath Robinson' affairs have been created by fishermen as an effective way of hauling their catch over the stones, some running for hundreds of yards, with their own bridges, viaducts and embankments. A variety of home-made motive power was used to pull them.

There were still around eight 'fish railways' evident at Dungeness at the turn of this century, but by 2009, most if not all of them had been discarded in favour of concrete or matting pathways to do the same job.

Of course, the most famous railway of all at Dungeness has to be the Romney, Hythe & Dymchurch Railway.

It was the brainchild of two men, racing driver, millionaire landowner, former Army Officer and miniature railway fan Captain Jack Howey and Count Louis Zborowski, a wealthy aristocrat who was also famous as a racing driver.

Zborowski wanted to build a fully working express railway in miniature. The locomotives would be scale replicas of main line steam locomotives, but would run on 15in gauge, not 4ft 8 1/2in.

The pair tried in vain to buy the Ravenglass & Eskdale Railway in the Lake District, a 15in gauge line laid on the trackbed of an earlier 3ft gauge freight operation.

Undeterred, Zborowski ordered two Pacific locomotives to be designed by the leading model railway engineer of his day, Henry Greenly, and built in Colchester by Davey, Paxman and Co, in anticipation of the day the pair would have a railway of their own on which to run them. They were named *Green Goddess*, after the 1921 stage play by William Archer which Howey had enjoyed, and *Northern Chief*.

However, Zborowski was killed while racing at Monza in the Italian Grand Prix before they could be delivered.

The captain was left with the two locomotives and finding a line on which to run them. Greenly came up with the idea of building a railway along the coast of Romney Marsh.

A double-track line was laid over the eight miles between Hythe and New Romney, the railway's headquarters, and the official opening took place on 16 July 1927, with another Pacific, *Hercules*, hauling the first train.

Howey extended the double tracks to Dungeness via Greatstone the following year.

The line was billed as the 'Smallest Public Railway in the World' and proved enormously popular. Soon there were nine miniature versions of main line express Pacific engines hauling a fleet of luxurious coaches.

Any notion that it was a 'toy' rather than 'real' railway were dispelled during World War Two, when it found itself in the front line of Britain's defence. Just as the Royal Military Canal had been built across the northern edge of Romney Marsh in 1810 to provide a line of defence should Napoleon's troops have landed, so the little railway found itself pressed into army service.

The War Department created the only miniature armoured train in the world as the line was used for patrols of the coast by the Somerset Light Infantry and there was extensive transport of soldiers on troop trains. The railway was also used extensively during the building of PLUTO (Pipe Line Under The Ocean) which fuelled the Allied invasion force following the D-Day landings in June 1944. ➤

Mallard it ain't: an abandoned fish railway locomotive as seen in August 2009. ROBIN JONES

Samson departs Dungeness with the modern lighthouse dating from 1961 in the background. ROBIN JONES

Look closely through the window of this very modern bungalow at Dungeness and you will see a railway carriage inside! ELSPETH THOMPSON

The railway was handed back to its owner after the end of the war, and the Hythe to New Romney section reopened to the public in 1946.

The New Romney to Dungeness section followed a year later with no less than Laurel and Hardy cutting the ribbon.

However, the war years had taken their tool, and the New Romney to Dungeness section had been reduced to single line only, as the raw materials to rebuild were scarce and the cost of reinstatement enormous.

With the growth of tourism along the Kent coast in the 50s and 60s, the railway greatly benefited, but as cheap package holidays abroad became readily available, less holidaymakers came and receipts fell.

Howey died in September 1963 with the lack of investment in the line already evident, a problem which was not fully addressed by subsequent owners. The rolling stock was ageing and giving rough rides, the locomotives were costly to maintain and carriages were in poor condition.

Samson heads towards Dymchurch with a service from Hythe on 29 August. ROBIN JONES

A Dungeness fish railway passes an abandoned hulk. ROBIN JONES

Multi-millionaire enthusiast Sir William McAlpine, who once owned Flying Scotsman, stepped in to reverse the downward trend in 1973, and since then, the railway has gone from strength to strength.

A main line should have a grand terminus, and in 1974, a new trainshed was erected over the New Romney platforms to give the impression of a major city terminus.

The fleet expanded in 1976 with German-built locomotive No 11 *Black Prince*, while all 10 original locomotives remain in service, covering thousands of miles each year. All well as the nine Pacifics and 4-8-2s, there was Krauss 0-4-0 tender tank locomotive No 4 which left the railway in 1926 after construction and ran in Belfast with the new name Jean. It returned to Romney in the 1970s and was restored in

the 1970s, and is known as The Bug. There are now a total of 16 locomotives.

Not only is the line a major tourist attraction, but also provides a public service between the small towns and villages between Hythe and Dungeness. Indeed, it was conceived as a public service, rather than a visitor attraction.

It is under contract to the local council to transport children to and from The Marsh Academy in New Romney. Local residents are transported to shopping centres and the railway has operated 'shoppers specials'. Holiday camp trains have operated with campers at Romney Sands and St Mary's Bay.

So while the 10 1/4in gauge Wells & Walsingham Light Railway in North Norfolk, laid along part of the Great Eastern Railway's Wells-next-the-Sea branch, has since 1982 claimed to be the world's

smallest public railway, the Romney line is still unique as a main line in miniature.

The railway's designers had also envisaged freight being carried, and that is partially why two of the original engines, No 5 Hercules and No 6 Samson were built to the Mountain 4-8-2 wheel arrangement because while lacking speed, they could haul heavy freight.

In 1937 a quarter-mile branch line was laid to the east of the main line near Dungeness, running to the beach, while platform one at Hythe was extended beside the station buildings and out to the front of the station. The purpose was to facilitate the movement of fish from Dungeness to Hythe for onward transportation by road.

The service was developed from 1937 following closure of the main line spur to Dungeness line that year. ➤

A fish railway viaduct over a dip in the famous shingle. ROBIN JONES

Green Goddess on the last lap on its journey to Hythe on 29 August. ROBIN JONES

The Romney line even went as far as to introduce its own fish wagons, but as a venture it took off in only a small way and was soon withdrawn. The venture, however, led to the idea of the above-mentioned fish railways at Dungeness.

The most successful freight service was the uncrushed ballast service. Also in 1937 a subsidiary ballast company was formed, with tipper wagons loaded with shingle from Dungeness beach taken along the fish branch and onwards to Hythe, where the contents were tipped into lorries from a ramp. The service lasted until 1951 when road transport took over.

The Romney railway is licensed by the Post Office for rail postal services, and is allowed to issue its own postage stamps. A four-wheel secure postage wagon was built, and several first-day covers have been issued.

The railway operates a parcels service, whereby parcels can be ferried from one station to another. The standard gauge line to New Romney & Littlestone-on-Sea once brought in coal for the little railway's engines. Devoid of a main line interchange for more than four decades, many have asked whether the railway could be extended.

In the late 1920s, there were plans for a two-mile extension with steep inclines from Hythe to Sandling to meet the Southern Railway at Sandling Junction; the gradients were another reason why the 4-8-2s were ordered. The plans fizzled out, but were briefly revisited in the 1980s when fresh surveys were compiled.

Since the railway was built, traffic levels on adjacent roads has increased many times over, and there have been several serious accidents on the line's 13 level crossings,

two of them in recent years fatal. While the crossings have been protected since the 1970s by flashing warning lights, all of them are having lifting half-barriers installed, just like the 'big' railway.

Howey wanted a railway that would last his lifetime. Those that built the Romney, Hythe & Dymchurch did much better: it is still a thriving concern in the modern age, long after the full-size steam locomotives which its engine fleet aimed to replicate were withdrawn from British Railway service.

Other 15in gauge railways have followed in its wake of its success, such as the Bure Valley Railway in Norfolk, the Cleethorpes Coast Light Railway in Lincolnshire. However, none of them can claim the history and pedigree of the railway that Jack built. ∎

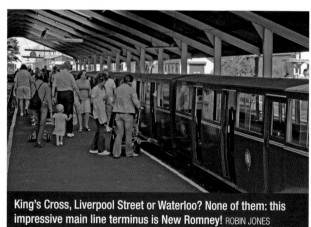

King's Cross, Liverpool Street or Waterloo? None of them: this impressive main line terminus is New Romney! ROBIN JONES

Captain Howey's favourite locomotive was *Hurricane* and remains a favourite of many visitors today thanks to its eye-catching Caledonian blue livery. It is seen at Hythe in 2008. MARK HEWITT

The preserved Post Office underground railway train inside the Great Hall at the National Railway Museum. ROBIN JONES

Rail Mail

London's 'other' underground was a miniature tube railway designed to carry tons of letters and parcels quickly and conveniently below the city's congested streets – until the Post Office decided it was cheaper to use the road after all!

For anyone interested in finding out more about Britain's railway heritage, the National Railway Museum in York is the first place to start.

The centrepiece is the Great Hall, where many of the headline-grabbing giants of the steam age are there on display, in pristine conditions – LNER A4 Pacific No 4468 *Mallard*, the world's fastest steam locomotive, a replica of Stephenson's Rocket, and the most recent addition, LMS Princess Coronation Pacific No 46229 *Duchess of Hamilton*, brilliantly restored to its as-built art deco streamlined condition by Bob Meanley's team at Tyseley Locomotive Works. One of the most popular exhibits is not British or steam at all, but a power car from the Japanese Bullet Train.

There is railway age glamour at every twist and turn.

However, one of the less conspicuous locomotive exhibits in the Great Hall, a former steam age roundhouse, is from one of Britain's most unusual yet most successful railways.

It is a train from London's famous Post Office underground railway. Unlike most of the museum locomotive and rolling stock exhibits, the general public will never have glimpsed it in operation at first hand.

Designed purely for the carriage of letters and parcels, this hidden 2ft gauge line, which ran in tunnels 70ft below the city's streets, ran for 19 hours a day, 286 days a year, on 23 miles of track.

It had no drivers or guards, and was fully automated, controlled in its latter years by computer.

At its height it carried over four million items of post a day, and managed to run over its six-and-a-half-mile main line from Paddington at one end to Whitechapel at the other in 26 minutes.

It had nine stations, the busiest being Mount Pleasant, serving two British Rail main line stations and major London sorting offices.

The idea of building an underground railway just to carry mail had its roots in 1853 when a 225-yard vacuum-operated tube just one-and-a-half inch in diameter went into service carrying letters.

The Post Office was impressed and looked into the potential that a much bigger system could offer. Six years later, the Pneumatic Dispatch Company built a test line at Battersea, followed by a tube from its headquarters next to the Post Office's North Western District Office to the parcel office at Euston station. It was followed by a second line from Euston to the General Post Office.

Receiving scant income, the company closed in 1874, but the idea was not forgotten.

Even at the dawn of the motor age in Edwardian times, congestion in the capital was nightmarish, and the Post Office needed a method other than road transport to transport mail between its city sorting offices. ➤

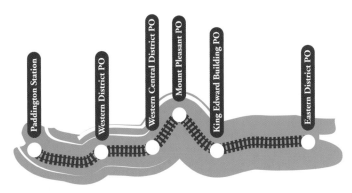

'Post Office Underground Mail Train: London', a GPO poster by Lili Rethi, c1950s, showing mail trains at an underground station being loaded and unloaded by Post Office workers. NRM

POST OFFICE UNDERGROUND MAIL TRAIN: LONDON

This atmospheric railcar dates from 1860 and is also in the care of the National Railway Museum at York. The idea for a pneumatic railway was devised by British inventor George Medhurst (1759-1827) in 1810. He proposed that a carriage containing goods or passengers could be blown along rails in an iron tube by the action of compressed air. The idea was revived in London 1860 by the Pneumatic Despatch Co for the transport of small goods, particularly mail. A 4ft diameter tunnel was built between Euston station and a district post office, with a later connection to the General Post Office. The venture eventually failed financially, but paved the way for the later Post Office underground railway. NRM

In 1908 a team of Post Office engineers visited the Chicago Freight subway system and a similar system in Berlin, Germany.

In Chicago, building of a subway system began in 1899, and by 1906 there was a tunnel under almost every downtown street. The 6ft wide and 7½ft high tunnels were officially constructed to house only telephone cables, but the Illinois Tunnel Company also secretly installed 2ft gauge railway tracks.

In 1911, the Post Office drew up a blueprint for a tunnel railway from Whitechapel to Paddington. Contractor John Mowlem & Co began tunnelling through the London clay in February 1915.

In 1917, work was suspended due to the shortage of labour and materials caused by World War One, and during the conflict the tunnels were used to house artworks from the Tate Gallery, National Portrait Gallery, British Museum and the Wallace Collection.

Tracklaying did not start until 1925, but progress was slowed down by the General Strike the following year.

While the main railway tunnel is 70ft below ground, the stations are constructed at a much shallower depth, giving a 1-in-20 gradient into and out of the station, so that

Mount Pleasant Post Office tube station in operation in 1996. NRM

A loaded Mail Rail train in 1997. NRM

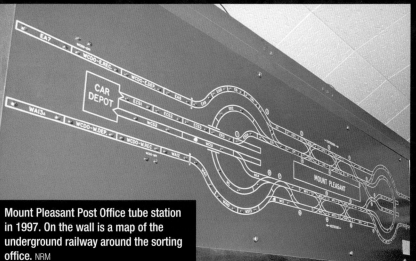

Mount Pleasant Post Office tube station in 1997. On the wall is a map of the underground railway around the sorting office. NRM

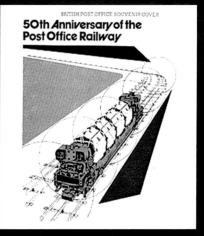

The 50th anniversary of the Post Office tube railway (1952-1977) was commemorated by a Royal Mail First Day Cover.

the mail had less distance to travel from the platforms to the surface, and to help slow the trains on their approach to the stations, and help acceleration away from them.

The trains took 440V DC power from a centre rail, allowing speeds of up to 40mph.

The first section, between Paddington and West Central District Office, was available for training in February 1927, and a year later, the first letter post was carried.

Kilmarnock Engineering provided 90 4wRE (RE stands for reference, the suffix 'RE' means, third rail-powered electric locomotive) four-wheeled units with English Electric traction equipment for use on the railway, in sets of three. However, they were found to be difficult and costly to operate, because their 7ft 3in wheelbase was unsuitable for the very tight curves led to regular derailments.

In 1929, after trials with an articulated car and a bogie car, an order was placed with English Electric for 50 bogie 2w-2-2-2wRE type units, and after early problems with them were solved, another 10 were ordered in 1936.

No more new traction units were built until 1962, when two new prototype units were ordered from English Electric. With the earlier stock needing replacement, 34 units were supplied by Greenbat and Hunslet between 1980-82.

During World War Two, the line was used as dormitories for post office staff.

In 1954, that because of problems of access at the Western District Office, Wimpole Street and the Western Central District Office, New Oxford Street, it was decided to build a new Western District Office at Rathbone Place, diverting the railway to run through the basement of the new office. While trains began running in 1958, it was not until seven years later that Postmaster General Anthony Wedgwood-Benn opened the new station and office.

In 1993, a £750,000 computer took over control of the system from one central point.

By 2003, only three stations remained in use because the sorting offices above the others had been relocated.

That year, Royal Mail announced that the underground railway was to be taken out of use because it was five times as expensive to send parcels and letters along it than to use alternative road transport.

The Communication Workers Union claimed the actual figure was closer to three times more expensive and argued that costs were high as a result of a policy of running the system down and using it at only one-third of its capacity. Despite a report by the Greater London Authority in support of Mail Rail, as the line was known since its 60th anniversary, the system was taken out of use on 31 May 2003.

Alternative used for the line were considered. At one stage it was suggested that despite its claustrophobic nature, it might even become a tourist attraction, but that idea was quickly dismissed as the costs were too high.

Many of the trains found new homes at other locations. In addition to the example at the NRM, they can be seen at venues as diverse as the Buckinghamshire Railway Centre, Amberley Museum in Sussex and the Launceston Steam Railway. ∎

Dinosaurs
from the underground

The Isle of Wight is world famous for the wealth of its prehistoric remains, and is home to Britain's first purpose-built dinosaur museum and visitor attraction. The island is considered the most important site for dinosaur remains in Europe, but who says they are extinct? Where else can you see obsolete London Transport tube trains running in the open next to the sea, under their own power, when most of their sister units have long since been scrapped?

The Isle of Wight has traditionally been a dumping ground for ageing locomotives. The pre-Grouping Isle of Wight Central Railway bought obsolete 'Terrier' 0-6-0 tank engines from the London Brighton & South Coast Railway, while the Southern Railway deployed veteran South Eastern & Chatham Railway O2 0-4-4Ts following the electrification of London suburban lines. These two classes in particular became synonymous with the island rail network up to the end of steam, which concerns us here.

The rail closures of the 60s were particularly unkind to Wight, which was left with just part of one route – the 8½-mile Ryde Pier to Shanklin section of the Ryde Pier-Ventnor line, serving the bigger resorts on the island's east coast.

It could have been worse: British Railways, had looked at closing the whole system after the 1964 holiday season apart from the Ryde Pier section, which would remain to link the ferry to a new bus station at Ryde Esplanade. When angry local residents, the Island Council and their MP protested, BR offered to keep Ryde-Shanklin open as a compromise. Many sceptics believed that it was what BR had wanted all along, and set a worse case scenario so it could be seen to be giving concessions.

In 1955, the British Railways Modernisation Plan decreed that steam should be phased out in favour of diesel and electric traction as soon as possible. The report, aimed at making the country's railways competitive once again, sparked a mad dash by manufacturers to turn out new forms of traction, some types of which were withdrawn either within a year or two of the final end of steam in 1968, or in some cases, even before it. Although the last railway on the Isle of Wight was physically detached from the network, it had to follow suit. But were the powers that be going to order a brand-new rolling stock fleet to run on it? No way – the old tradition of second-hand stock would be followed yet again.

However, this time it would not be redundant tank engines, but electric trains – from London Underground.

Steam trains were withdrawn from Ryde Pier on 17 September, and the whole line on 31 December 1966. The closure of the line to allow electrification to take place provided the opportunity to raise the height of the trackbed in Esplanade Tunnel, to reduce flooding by very high tides and eliminate the need for costly pumping out of water afterwards. Tube trains rather than Southern Region electric multiple units were therefore ideal. Their low clearances designed to fit the headroom of the underground allowed them to fit perfectly inside the Esplanade Tunnel.

A vintage 1938 tube train restored to its London Transport livery still gives sterling services on the Island Line. SOUTH WEST TRAINS

Above left: **As it was before the line was electrified: O2 class 0-4-4T No 33 *Bembridge* in service at Ryde St Johns.** COLOUR-RAIL

Above: **One of the first generation of redundant tube trains on the Island Line, this BR blue-liveried Class 485 unit stands at Ryde Pier Head station.** COLOUR-RAIL

Two 1938 tube stock units carrying 'dinosaur' livery pass at Sandown in April 2001. ROBIN JONES

After more than 70 years, London Underground 1938 stock tube trains are still running – but not in the capital! SOUTH WEST TRAINS

Second-hand rolling stock has always found a ready home on the Isle of Wight. LSSCR 'Terrier' tank W8 *Freshwater*, typical of a class which, like the tube trains, enjoyed a second life on the island, is seen in action on the Isle of Wight Steam Railway. IoWSR

The southern section of the line, from Shanklin to Ventnor, closed in April 1966. Most people remain surprised that such a short length was not saved, bearing in mind that Ryde-Shanklin was to remain open and that Ventnor is also a sizeable holiday destination. The Southern Region claimed it was very unprofitable, but it was later claimed that BR did not want to go to the expense of building an additional electric sub station, secretly intending the close the Ryde-Shanklin line within a few years.

While the line was closed, the rebuilding of Ryde Pier Head station was completed and Ryde Esplanade station was substantially modified. The line reopened on 20 March 1967 following its electrification, with platform heights adjusted to accommodate the tube trains.

The first trains were electrical multiple units originally built for the London Electric Railway from 1923-31 as Standard tube stock. They were bought by British Rail from London Underground in 1967 and six four-cars were refurbished by Stewarts Lane depot in 1966-67. To place them in perspective, at the same time, one was sent to the Science Museum!

The units were initially classified Class 452 and numbered 041-046, later reclassified Class 485 and numbered 485041-046. Each unit was formed of a driving motor, two intermediate trailers, and a second driving motor.

At first, the units carried all-over BR blue livery with the double arrow logo.

This changed to standard blue/grey livery in the 1970s, and some units received Network SouthEast's blue livery with red and white stripes, in 1986.

Following the Southern Region's numerical classification for EMU types, the four-car sets became 4VEC, and three-car sets 3TIS. When they ran together to make a seven-coach train, they became VECTIS, the Roman name for the Isle of Wight.

Surprisingly, residents warmed to the ageing units, which had been overhauled and smartened up.

Also, the electrification allowed the line speed to be raised from 40mph to 45mph, giving a more frequent services both at peak and off-peak times. While they were perfect for negotiating the lowered clearance of the tunnel, they fared badly in the salt sea air. Out of the city tunnels and exposed to the full force of the elements, they suffered badly from corrosion damage on the island. ➤

Above: **The dinosaur livery was both striking and apart in more ways than one.**
ROBIN JONES

Left: **A 1938 tube train glides along Ryde Pier.** KEITH SKUCE

By the mid-80s, it was obvious that the Class 485s needed replacing, with residents complaining frequently about rough riding. Again, because of the low clearance issue, London Underground stock was sought again, in the form of Metro-Cammell 1938 tube stock, with 20 cars secured.

The 485s were extensively refurbished between 1989-92 by Eastleigh Works in readiness for a new lease of life on Wight after half a century in the capital.

Significant electrical works were required both to replace dilapidated wiring, and to allow the units to work from the line's third rail electrical supply.

The first unit was tested on the South West Main Line between Basingstoke and Eastleigh, while testing and crew training on the others took place on the Portsmouth Direct Line and Shepperton branch.

They were introduced from 1989 as Class 483 two-car sets, running in formations of up to three pairs, with the last 485s withdrawn from service in 1992. Five 485 vehicles were sold back to London Underground for eventual restoration as part of an operational Standard stock museum heritage unit. In 1989, the last 1938 stock was withdrawn from London Underground, the

final five sets in service having been required to work Northern Line trains until then.

In 1996, with the privatisation of Britain's railways, the Ryde-Shanklin line became the Island Line franchise, which was won by the Stagecoach Group. Services continued to be branded as Island Line.

In the late 1990s, several 485s were as surplus to requirements and withdrawn from service. From 2000 onwards, the remaining five units were overhauled, and most repainted into a new livery of blue and yellow… with pictures of dinosaurs on the sides – reflecting the geological riches of Wight, and ironically the nature of the electric fleet. The fleet was later repainted into the original London Transport red livery, with the additional of yellow warning panels on the cab.

There have been regular calls for the line south of Shanklin to Ventnor to be reopened. Other proposals for the future of the railway have included conversion of the line to an express bus road, rebuilding it as a light rail tram system and even linking the line to the mainland network via a tunnel beneath The Solent. Indeed, talks about a tunnel took place as early 1886, and in 1901, parliamentary powers for a railway

beneath the Solent were obtained, but the scheme failed to raise sufficient capital.

In 2007, the Island Line franchise was amalgamated with South West Trains as part of the new South Western Franchise. Despite the availability of newer redundant underground stock, in 2009 there were no plans to acquire fresh units to replace the 485s. Long may the dinosaurs live.

At the midway station of Smallbrook Junction, passengers can change trains for the Isle of Wight Steam Railway, which runs on five miles of the old Ryde-Newport line from there as far as Wootton.

The steam line has a wonderful collection of old wooden-bodied carriages restored to pristine condition after being used as bungalows or outbuildings on the island, hauled by locomotives historically appropriate to the island. It is a classic heritage railway, but there again, surely the Island Line with its veteran stock falls into that category too?

The unusual sight of undergroundtrains running on an island is not unique to Wight.

On the two-mile Alderney Railway in the Channel Islands, two examples of 1956 tube stock are hauled by diesel shunters to make up passenger trains. ∎

Above: **The interior of one of the 1938 underground cars.** KEITH SKUCE

Right: **A Railway Clearing House map of the Isle of Wight lines at their height.** ROBIN JONES COLLECTION

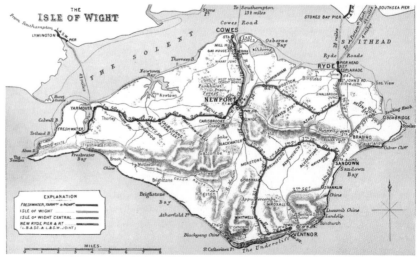

A garden railway
— in broad gauge!

Building a model railway in the back garden has been a popular pastime for many enthusiasts. Many have electric-powered OO or O gauge systems, while others have built live steam miniature lines which offer passenger rides through the flowerbeds. However, a house in Berkshire has goner one better than the rest – for it now has a garden railway where both the locomotive and track are BIGGER than its full-size British counterparts!

Back in 1951, the first of 999 British Railways Standard steam locomotives was outshopped, in the form of Britannia Pacific No 70000 *Britannia*. For crews, passengers and the army of schoolboy trainspotters to be found everywhere on the national network, they were the ultimate in glamour power.

Two years later, a young schoolboy named David Buck had the privilege of 'cabbing' one in the form of No 70035 *Rudyard Kipling* at Ipswich station. The locomotive was on display to raise funds for the relief appeal for the east coast floods in February 1953. David grew up near the East Suffolk line to Lowestoft, and regularly watched the Claud Hamiltons, J15s and L1s in action on local lines.

His dad Peter founded the Hornby Railway Society in Ipswich in 1929 and David still has the framed certificate.

David had his own trainset back then, and he still does today – in fact he has two.

He went on to become a hugely successful businessman outside the field of railways, as managing director of a company which processes movie film for the likes of 20th Century Fox, but his passion for steam never died one bit.

In 1981, he bought a luxury half-timbered house which had previously been home to the late eccentric hairdresser 'Teasier Weasie' Raymond in a village near Windsor and began building a 3½in gauge live steam railway on land at the back.

After a few years, with the circuit up and running, he decided to go up in the world, and build a 4ft 8½in standard gauge railway.

Full-size private garden railways are not in themselves a scarcity. Multi-millionaire enthusiast Sir William McAlpine's extensive standard-gauge line at his Fawley Hill home in Berkshire is well known; while Chiltern Railways supremo Adrian Shooter has a 2ft gauge line, the Beeches Light Railway, with a former Darjeeling

David Buck today – at home in the cab of his own Pacific, slightly bigger than a *Britannia*! ROBIN JONES

Himalayan Railway Sharp Steward B class 0-4-0 saddle tank providing the motive power, hauling a pair of replica coaches of the legendary Indian line built by the Ffestiniog Railway workshops at Boston Lodge.

The best-known full-size garden railway was the late Rev Teddy Boston's Cadeby Light Railway at his rectory in the Leicestershire village of the same name, which had a short 2ft gauge line in the garden. ➤

David Buck on the footplate of then brand-new Britannia Pacific No 70035 *Rudyard Kipling* at Ipswich in 1963. DAVID BUCK COLLECTION

Finnish Hr1 class 4-6-2 No 1016 *Lady Patricia* has been bought to restore to steam in deepest Berkshire. ROBIN JONES

The pride of David's fleet, classic Peckett saddle tank *Hornpipe*. ROBIN JONES

His collection was sold off by his widow in recent years and the line, opened to the public once a month, sadly is no more.

Two years ago, however, David went one better, and acquired a 5ft gauge Finnish 4-6-2. Not only is the track gauge three-and-a-half inches wider than that used on the British network since Stephenson won the day against Brunel's 7ft 0¼in, but the locomotive is taller and wider than British Pacifics: it is 'the next size up' from *Flying Scotsman*.

The locomotive was acquired from British businessman Nigel Sill, who runs heritage steam excursions in Finland. In the 80s, he imported several Finnish steam locomotives to Britain for a Wild West theme park in Cornwall whoseplans to build a railway never took off,and the locomotives were left to be stored in various places around Essex and North London.

The one David bought, Hr1 class No 1016, had been on static display at Enfield for some years. Built in 1955, it was one of a class of 22 built in Finland by Tampella and Lokomo between 1937 and 1957. They were the biggest passenger locomotives built or used in Finland and remained the main locomotives used for southern Finland on express trains until 1963, when Hr12 class diesels took over. Along with the German Class 10s, the Hr1s were the last new-built Pacifics built in Europe before the end of the steam age.

After dieselisation, several Finnish steam engines were stored at the Lievestuore military depot near Haapamäki to be used during times of crisis, when diesel oil would be hard to come by. The engines were packaged and protected against rusting and weather until the 80s, when a decision was made to dispose of them.

While No 1016 has yet to steam in preservation, in summer 2009, David was carrying out a major retubing operation, after which he believes the locomotive will return to steam.

He has laid a 300-yard running line for it to move up and down. The massive tender will have a wooden deck fitted at the rear, above the coal container, and seats will be fitted so passengers will be able to ride on it.

In the meantime, the locomotive, now named *Lady Patricia*, is floodlit at night, so David can enjoy the sight of his own main line Pacific from his bedroom window.

Unlike other preserved steam locomotives, it will never be hired to other railways, because nobody else in Britain has a 5ft gauge running line.

It is unlikely to become as extensive as his standard gauge line, which has been extended to form a pear-shaped loop.

Little and large: *Hornpipe* and *Lady Patricia* line up together. ROBIN JONES

Another private railway in Berkshire is construction magnate Sir William McAlpine's line at his Fawley Hill residence, pictured with visiting London & South Western railway Beattie 2-4-0 well tank No 30587 in action recreating the Wenfordbridge freight branch in Cornwall. Passengers are likely to glimpse wallabies which roam freely in the ground (INSET). ROBIN JONES

His first standard gauge locomotive was *Hornpipe*, Peckett 0-4-0 saddle tank No 1756 of 1928 *Hornpipe*, which spent its entire working life at a chalk quarry near Holborough in Kent, owned by a cement manufacturer.

It arrived at the Buckinghamshire Railway Centre from a scrapyard in 1972 and was restored to haul passenger trains, and sold on to David in 1985.

Lengths of track were salvaged from various parts of Britain, including five points from the GWR Swindon Works which closed in 1986. It was followed by Hawthorn Leslie 0-6-0ST No 3138 of 1916, a former Corby steelworks engine, a long-term restoration project, and GWR 'Toad' brake van No 14748, which dates from 1942 and formed the line's first passenger train.

Another exile from Buckinghamshire Railway Centre now in David's possession is Aveling & Porter flywheel-driven four-wheeler No 8800 of 1917 *Sir Vincent*, which saw industrial service in Erith in Kent. Five standard gauge Aveling & Porter locomotives survive in preservation; their appearance quickly shows that they have much in common with traction engines. David bought it after a bid to restore a part of the Brill Tramway – which used such locomotives – at the centre's Quainton Road base fell flat. A converted wagon with drop sides has been fitted with two GWR station benches, and forms an open carriage for trips along the line, which now has several level crossings.

A sizeable workshop which would do justice to many a heritage railway has

been erected for the maintenance of the rolling stock, and houses a four-wheel Barclay diesel obtained from the Rutland Railway Museum. The line is never opened to the general public, but has hosted visits from groups like the Industrial Railway Society.

"One of the reasons why I bought the house before the property prices went up in the 1980s was that it had so much flat land, a garden railway could be built," said David.

"The 5in gauge line was so much fun that I considered a full-size line and thought – why not? We had the space.

"A chap I knew asked me if I would show him how to drive *Hornpipe*, and offered a weekend riding in his 'old plane' in exchange. I agreed – and his 'old plane' turned out to be a Lear jet. We had a tremendous time flying all round Europe on it, while he learned to drive my steam engine. He reckoned that he had the better of the bargain."

As for the broad gauge addition, he said: "The locomotive was kept as part of the Finnish strategic reserve and the boiler is in superb condition.

"You could not buy a British standard gauge Pacific, but I will soon have an even bigger 4-6-2 of my own running."

Peter is now part of the North British Locomotive Preservation Group, which aims to build two examples of the Gresley B17 4-6-0s, the 'Sandringham' and 'Footballer' classes from scratch, one for use both on the main line and heritage railways, and the other for static display and a source of spare parts. Who knows – one might even undergo its test runs in the back garden! ∎

Aveling & Porter 'traction engine' locomotive *Sir Vincent* in action. ROBIN JONES

The forgotten railways of
Seagull Island

From the mainland, Steep Holm island appears to be a little more lump of rock in the middle of the Bristol Channel. Yet it once boasted not only its own railway, but a complete system with two separate lines – much of which are still in place today, in a place which is a unique and magical blend of historical artefacts and the natural world and is well worth making the voyage.

Somerset after the last Ice Age: a chain of limestone hills we now know as the Mendips stretched as far as South Glamorgan, perforated by a river winding its way through thick forests to a distant sea.

Over the centuries, as icecaps melted and glaciers receded, the sea rose, eventually swamping the valley and the forests.

The river became an ocean all of its own, the Severn Sea, the sweeping estuary of the longest watercourse on the British mainland. The outliers of the Mendips found themselves turned into islands, either in the great marshlands that are now the Somerset levels, or in the case of the westernmost pair, out at sea.

What had been a great valley had been turned into a funnel directly facing the Atlantic breakers. Every day the surge of the surf pushes the waters of the Severn estuary back up the funnel, creating the second biggest tidal range in the world after Canada's Bay of Fundy. At low water, vast expanses of sand and mudflats on the Somerset coast are laid bare, quickly covered again as the sediment-laden brown waters rush in when the tide turns.

The two Mendip outliers, Steep and Flat Holm, stand in the middle of the estuary as unlike twins, shaped exactly as their names suggest.

Appearing as mere lumps of grass-topped rock when viewed from either shore, to many it seems inconceivable that anyone would have ever wanted to inhabit either of them. Yet both have a history dating back thousands of years – indeed, it is believed that St Gildas wrote the first history of Britain while staying Steep Holm in the sixth century.

Not only that, but both had operational railways – and in the case of Steep Holm, an unlikely railway network!

I say 'had' – because Flat Holm, which has been part of Wales since the Norman Conquest, lost its line to the scrapmen soon after it became redundant. Yet Steep Holm proved to steep for them to tackle: quite simply, the time and expense that would be incurred in scaling its heights could never justify the reclamation of scrap rails and metal sleepers. More than 60 years after it saw its last train movements, the little railway is still there for all to see – a perfect case of preservation, if only because nobody wants to lift its rusting tracks.

The Kenneth Allsop Memorial Trust, which has managed the island as a nature reserve in honour of the late broadcaster and naturalist since 1974, runs trip boats on selected days from Knightstone Harbour at Weston-super-Mare.

The trips aboard the Bristol Queen have to dovetail in perfectly between the tides, which afford only a small window of opportunity for the island's landing beach to be used. Not only that, but an early start often has to be made, and the boat will sail northwards up the estuary away from the island on the outward journey. It is the only way that it can tackle the force of the tidal surge, the forces that have inspired the clamour in recent decades for a Severn barrage to be built to harness its energy. When sufficiently upstream, the boat will ride with the current towards the island, often making a circular tour of it before the beach is reached. The trip is an exhilarating experience in itself.

After alighting on the shingle East Beach, you immediately become aware than humans are no longer in charge of the island. Nature has long since reclaimed it; you may climb the zig-zag incline path to the top and follow the routes around the summit, inspect the sheer wealth of military structures from two world wars and an earlier conflict which never happened, take lunch in the World War Two barracks now converted into a dining room and souvenir shop, but be warned – you are not in control.

With humans occupying it only during day trips, and there being no permanent residency, seagulls are the undisputed masters of the 63-acre island now. ➤

Somerset's Steep Holm island, as viewed from the huge shingle spit which appears off East Beach at low water. ROBIN JONES

Left: The island pub that was partially demolished to make way for the railway. A harbour built at the same time as the inn was washed away in 1860. Middle: Landing on Steep Holm today can only be done at precise states of the tide. Right: The site of one of the winding houses which hauled the trains up the zig-zag path. ALL ROBIN JONES

The railway track still in place on the zig-zag incline path. The sleepers have been covered with soil to make it easier for the island's Honda Power Carrier to take supplies to the summit. ROBIN JONES

'Her attacker was a huge grizzly bear which was chained to a kennel inside the premises, which Fred had obtained in exchange for his guard dog.'

Every sound sequence in a seagull's vocabulary, and you will soon find that there are enough of them to give the impression of a language, will be shrieked over and over again.

If you inadvertently approach their nests or chicks which are to be found in the middle of the island summit's footpaths – there are no natural predators, and they breed anywhere without fear – you will be told in no uncertain terms you are not welcome. The standard practice is to dive at you directly from the front or rear, and then apply wing uplift seconds before contact, so you just feel the jet stream from the ferocious flapping passing fractionally over your head. The deafening shrieks of tens of thousands of seagulls which make the island their sanctuary quickly reinvoke Alfred Hitchcock's The Birds at every step. Indeed, Steep Holm is a world apart from the mainland civilisation in so many respects, and it is an experience to be prized.

Then there are the alexanders, a yellow-flowering herb popular as a celery substitute in medieval times. When you visit in early spring, it seems that the plant has taken over almost every square inch. To walk round the island you have to hack your way through alexanders which have grown several feet high. Their seeds get everywhere, inside your clothes, up your nose, in your mouth. You live, breathe and taste alexanders while you visit the island, and never want to see one or sense their unmistakeable aroma ever again!

From East Beach, there is one way up to the top of the island, which was once home to a small 12th-century colony of monks and a farmhouse, and that is up a natural incline in

the limestone strata which as a result of primeval earth movements tilts at 30 degrees to the horizontal. It conveniently forms both a path – and a trackbed for a railway.

The first question every visitor asks is how did this all but uninhabited lump of rock end up not only with its own railway – but two separate lines?

The answer lies in the two world wars.

Following the evacuation of the British Army from Dunkirk in 1940, Britain was placed on invasion alert. Fortifications were erected at every conceivable 'weak' point across the country, with special emphasis given to the southern coastline facing the English Channel. Other areas, however, could have been equally vulnerable, and the docks at Cardiff and Newport were particularly vulnerable to Luftwaffe raids.

The Holms were not only the guardians of the shipping lane leading to the Port of Bristol but also stood below the flight path of bombers. They also afforded protection to the Atlantic convoys which would rendezvous in the Bristol Channel.

Somerset was also considered particular vulnerable to a potential invasion because of the flat levels, over which an invading force might quickly make ground, and so it was turned into a fortress, bristling with pillboxes and gun emplacements.

Both islands were taken over by the Army and again turned into fortresses. I say 'again' because both islands were already covered by an extensive series of fortifications dating from the 1860s when unfounded fears of the intentions of the French Emperor Napoleon III, a nephew of Bonaparte,

prompted the British Government under Lord Palmerston to commission a new chain of defensive forts to be built around the coast of southern England.

Thankfully no shot was fired in anger. In fact, Napoleon III was rather fond of England and spent his last years in exile here after his country's humiliating defeat in the Franco-Prussian War of 1870-71 and the island forts, including the barracks on Steep Holm, were eventually vacated in 1902.

Steep Holm's 10 massive 7in muzzle loading cannons were left to the devices of the scrap merchants; however, because of the topography of the island, no-one considered their salvage worthwhile, and nine have survived intact.

As air raids began on British cities, Mk VII 6in breech loading guns up to 40 years old were hurriedly taken from ammunition stores in Cardiff by the Royal Artillery Regiment for use on the islands.

A contingent of Indian Army soldiers with mule teams arrived, the animals carrying much of the equipment up the incline path to the summit.

Building supplies and equipment were brought in by tank landing craft prior to the construction of a jetty at Last Beach, an essential amenity. The sheer extent of the planned island fortifications meant that the Indian sappers' mule trains using the single narrow incline path up from the beach would prove inadequate if the gun emplacements were to be completed in time to be effective against the growing number of air raids. As far as the military engineers were concerned, the only answer was to build a railway.

Track materials which had been held in store at the Longmoor Military Railway since World War One were brought to the island.

It is generally believed that the components had been previously used in trench lines on the Western Front; David Benger, battery commander on Flat Holm from 1941-44, said he understood that the rail at least was of German origin and had been 'captured' from the Huns in 1918.

Royal Engineers worked round the clock to build a 120ft-long girder landing jetty, standing waist deep in the freezing brown sea to complete it, as a permanent harbour that was not reliant on the precarious state of tides was necessary.

Then a formation had to be created to take the railway from the new military harbour up the zig-zag incline path to the plateau at the island's summit. A fisherman's cottage and a pub which dated from 1832 and had drawn its trade from sailors on passing ships waiting to enter the port of Bristol were largely blasted away by explosives laid by 930 Port Construction and Repair Company to make way for the railway.

As an aside, the publican in the mid-19th century, Fred Harris, who had skirmishes with Somerset magistrates over the opening hours, found himself at the centre of a claim for damages in 1858. Teacher Ann Besozzi took out a civil action against him for injuries suffered when she was felled to the floor by an almighty blow to the back.

The World War Two Meccano-style pier at East Beach being demolished in 1946. This is the only known picture of the island railway in its operational days. Only the rusting pier stanchions survive today. Several of the trucks are seen on the railway line. KAMT

Her attacker was a huge grizzly bear which was chained to a kennel inside the premises, which Fred had obtained in exchange for his guard dog. A fellow visitor succeeded in fighting off the bear with his umbrella which was broken into pieces in the process. Miss Besozzi required extensive treatment for severe injuries. In his defence, Harris said that the bear regularly played with his children like an ordinary family dog and was a docile creature.

The railway, comprising rails fixed to metal sleepers, was built in 1941 as a cable-operated incline line in separate sections laid on the zig-zag path. It was constructed to 1ft 11½in gauge, the same as the Ffestiniog Railway.

At the top of each of the three sections was a set of points and a diesel-operated winch house. Trucks were loaded on the jetty using a diesel crane. They were coupled together to the front truck. The train was then hauled up the inclines by each winch in turn, reversing at the end of each zig-zag section.

The 1-in-2/3 gradient of the path caused problems for the trucks, which each had an 8cwt (406 kg) capacity. The profiles of the rails were accordingly bent in at least five places with oxyacetylene torches to provide greater adhesion.

At the top of the incline, a long-forgotten diesel locomotive, possibly a Hunslet 0-4-0, hauled the wagons to the various construction sites and sidings around the plateau, as was the case on the sister railway on Flat Holm, ➤

The start of the incline path over which the railway ran, the ruined pub to the right. ROBIN JONES

Above: Hated by World War Two soldiers, the Victorian barracks now house a shop and dining facilities for visitors. ROBIN JONES

Top: The interior of the barracks. ROBIN JONES

A sketch of anti-aircraft guns in action on adjacent Flat Holm, which had its island military railway removed for scrap after World War Two because of the far greater ease of access. ROBIN JONES

A Victorian cannon lies on top on the island inside the battery built for it. As with the railway, scrapmen did not consider reclamation economically justifiable. ROBIN JONES

former sergeant Joe Walford later recounted. Other reports said that the wagons on the summit line were either pulled by mules or pushed by hand. The full extent of the track, believed to have been about two-thirds-of-a-mile, remains unclear.

Once operational, the line carried vast quantities of sand and cement for the military building sites. A new set of four gun batteries superseded the Palmerston era originals and searchlight positions, generator houses and a battery observation post were also constructed at different points around the summit of the 256ft high island.

After the emplacements had been finished and the heavy guns delivered, much of the rail 'network' on the top of the island became redundant and was lifted, with Nissen huts being built on part of the formation. The incline section, however, remained in use for the delivery of ammunition and general supplies.

Fears that rough weather or storm surges would render the East Beach jetty unusable led to a second landing stage being built below the cliffs to the south.

South Landing, as it was called, was also served by a winch-operated railway linking it to the path which circuits the summit of the island, although this line appears to have been

seldom if ever used. With care, in dry weather, that path and the second railway can be followed today by visitors.

At one stage more than 200 men were based on Steep Holm, preparing the guns for action at any time of the day. Parachute mines dropped by Nazi planes in the Bristol Channel were often seen floating in the waters off the island; indeed, several ships from Avonmouth were blown up by them.

Occasionally, German bombers flew low past Steep Holm on their way to Cardiff and, frustratingly, the island's anti-aircraft guns could not be lowered sufficiently to hit them.

Wartime conditions on the island were said to be very harsh, with an acute lack of water (a washing bowl had to be shared by 12 men) a typhoid outbreak, a ban on eating gulls' eggs for risk of infection, and blackout conditions which led to several men falling over the cliffs, not to mention the often-inhospitable channel climate.

A 40mm Bofors anti-aircraft gun. Six were positioned on Steep Holm during World War Two. ROBIN JONES

Soldiers who were ferried over to the island for tours of duty cheered loudly when the sea became too choppy for them to land and they had to be taken back to Cardiff.

It was not always Cardiff that took a pounding. Weston-super-Mare emerged as a prime target for bombers on 28 June 1942, just days after the News Chronicle had run a front-page splash with the boastful headline 'Weston does not know there is a war on'. Despite wartime austerity, holidaymakers continued to visit Weston and the hot summer that year brought the crowds back; unlike most other beaches, Weston's main sandy beach was not mined or protected by rows barbed wire. A display of military hardware was staged on the sea front for munitions factory workers from all over Britain and the newspaper carried a photograph of the event.

The paper's front page turned out be a red rag to an insane bull.

While most air raids over the Holms had come from the Somerset direction, the one that began that evening came unexpectedly from the sea. Air sirens were never sounded as the town was left totally unprepared, and the inhabitants did not even have time to scurry into their Anderson shelters.

Air raids from the west had not been anticipated: the distinctive white far end of Weston's Grand Pier was not camouflaged and it gave the Nazi pilots duly aided by a glorious full moon, an added navigational bonus.

Around 100 high-explosive bombs and 1000 incendiaries were dropped on the resort over two nights, several planes flying so low that they passed streets at the height of first-floor windows machine-gunning everything below. While initially released figures put the death toll at 102 with 400 more injured, many locals believed the true numbers were much higher.

After the raids, Nazi sympathiser William Joyce, nicknamed Lord Haw Haw, who broadcast German propaganda nightly to Britain on Radio Hamburg, gloated: "I presume Weston knows there is a war on."

Above: **The huge concrete batteries at the eastern end of the island.** ROBIN JONES

Right: **Looking down the incline towards the South Landing.** ROBIN JONES

Piles of reclaimed rails are stacked above East Beach. ROBIN JONES

A set of wheels from an island railway truck are displayed inside the museum next to the barracks. ROBIN JONES

The winch at the top of the South Incline. ROBIN JONES

However, following D-Day in June 1944, the threat of Nazi invasion quickly diminished and all defence units were run down. Steep Holm was no exception and closed down later that year.

German prisoners of war were used to dismantle much of the fortifications including the East Beach jetty. Captured German NCO Max Hemming later remarked that the railway outlived the guns and searchlights, and his group not only used the line to carry supplies but passengers too!

The weight of the trucks was all that was needed to take them back down, with a brake on the winch acting as a safeguard, the PoWs found to their delight. Once, however. when nobody bothered to operate the brake, a truck ran down out of control, left the track and somersaulted on to the beach.

It seems that became the fate of other wagons, for while none today survive intact, a set of wheels was found off South Landing in 1977, and three more sets were salvaged from the sea off the western end of the island during a very low tide seven years later.

After Germany's defeat, it was the turn of Lord Haw Haw to get his come-uppance. Shot in the backside by British troops during his arrest, the bullet had to be removed by a Dr Corcos – a Weston general practitioner who was only too aware of the casualties inflicted on his home town. Joyce was later hanged for treason.

Abandoned by the military, and unwanted by the scrapmen, the little railway was left to rust.

When the Kenneth Allsop Memorial Trust took over the island, one of the first tasks was to clear vegetation from the incline path. The Department of the Environment has also advised that the railway track should stay intact because of its historic importance.

However, while the possibility was tempting for many reasons, it was realised any restoration of the line to working order would immediately place it in potential conflict with pedestrians. A runaway truck on a cable-hauled railway would take no prisoners on the narrow incline. As there is no realistic alternative path for visitors, the railway must therefore stay closed.

In recent times the railway track has been partially buried to allow the trust's Honda Power Carrier to use the incline without risk of its caterpillar tracks becoming damaged.

Burial is also limiting the corrosive power of the salt air, which is already visibly taking its toll on many of the metal sleepers which are crumbling to dust.

However, it would be superb if the trust was to restore a part of the line, maybe a winding house and a set of pointwork at the end of a zig-zag section, for static display, and perhaps this will happen when precious funds permit.

However, it is all but certain that this forgotten but fascinating outpost of railway heritage will never see train movements again, and through necessity, it is set to remain dormant until the effects of the elements take their final toll.

*Anyone wishing to visit Steep Holm and see its unique railway relics are invited to contact the Kenneth Allsop Memorial Trust to make prior bookings, which are essential.

Telephone 01934 522125 or email steepholmbookings@fsmail.net

The fares are £25 for adults and £12.50 for children, part of which goes towards maintaining the island, and the author fully recommends the trip. ■

The company's 25th anniversary at Seaton saw an Edwardian-style terminus built in the town, seen here with three trams in service. SEATON TRAMWAY

Forget the train - take the tram!

Many seaside branch lines were closed in the 1960s, and despite the fact that the car had become king, the resorts they had served nonetheless suffered declining fortunes as a result. However, to quote Shakespeare, one such branch underwent a sea change into something rich and strange — and successfully re-emerged phoenix-like as a tramway.

It would have been marvellous if the string of seaside resorts that sprang up along the shore of East Devon and West Dorset could have been served by a single main line railway. However, the hilly topography did not allow it, and the London & South Western railway main line from London to Exeter had to run a few miles inland somewhat parallel to coast.

The coast was served by a series of delightful short branches running south from the main line to ancient ports and small fishing settlements – Exmouth, Budleigh Salterton, Sidmouth, Lyme Regis, and Seaton.

A steam-hauled auto train hauled by GWR 0-4-2T No 1442 leaves Colyton for Seaton on 27 February 1965 during the twilight years of the railway. PETER W GRAY

Car 12 prepares to depart Colyton. ROBIN JONES

The magnificent Exeter Car 19 in Riverside Depot. ROBIN JONES

End of the road: Car 9 pulls up to the buffer stops at Colyton, beyond which the old trackbed of the railway branch led to Seaton Junction station on the London-Exeter main line. There are no current plans by the tramway operator to rebuild that section, but many visitors still ask about the possibility. ROBIN JONES

It was the arrival of the Seaton & Beer Railway in 1868 which turned Seaton into a busy holiday resort, and it was the post-Beeching closure of the branch line on 7 March 1966, which dealt a blow to its seasonal trade. While around 1200 passengers rode on the line on summer Saturdays, less than a dozen were there to make the final trip that winter.

The route of the old branch railway is still, however, reverberating to the sound of steel wheels. They do not belong to trains in the conventional sense, but traditional British street trams, a typical sight in city streets throughout the country in the first half of the 20th century.

What's more, there is something very unusual about these trams. Several of them are genuine trams from the last century, but they have been dismantled and cut down to size, to make them about two thirds as big as the originals.

No longer do they ply their trade through urban roads, but alongside the beautiful unspoilt estuary of the River Axe which is famous for its birdlife.

Here is the single feature which makes Seaton different from anywhere else in Britain today. ➤

The age-old tradition of bright floral displays on station platforms is maintained at Colyton. ROBIN JONES

Birdwatching from the upper deck of the open-top trams is one of the principal attractions of the tramway. SEATON TRAMWAY

Trams passing on a loop. ROBIN JONES

Driver at the controls. SEATON TRAMWAY

'The tramway now has extraordinary varieties of vehicle from open double-deckers and basic wooden seats to luxuriously upholstered wood-panelled cars.'

The Seaton Tramway has its origins in a manufacturer of milk floats and other battery-electric vehicles. Claude Lane, owner of the Lancaster Electrical Company in Barnet, North London, had a passion for trams and at his factory in 1949 he had built a 15in gauge tram based on ex-Darwen Car 23, then running on the Llandudno & Colwyn Bay system.

Hugely popular as an attraction at fetes, Claude was surprised by its popularity. He ran it for a summer season at St Leonards, Sussex, in 1951 and for five seasons at Rhyl from 1952.

He decided to lease a permanent site at Eastbourne in 1953, and set up Modern Electric Tramways Ltd to operate it.

His 2ft gauge Eastbourne Electric Tramway ran for two-thirds of a mile between Princes Park and the Crumbles and his factory made a larger open-top tram, Car 6, also based on the open-top design of Llandudno & Colwyn Bay vehicles, to run on it. It was followed in 1958 by the similar Car 8, in 1961 by Car 4, which was based on a Blackpool Tramways 'open boat' design, and in 1964 by Car 2, based on a London Metropolitan Tramways design.

The growth of Eastbourne's road system began to squeeze the tramway out and Claude began looking for a freehold site.

He heard about the imminent fate of the Seaton branch tenure and eventually British Railways agreed to sell, on condition he received a Transfer Order and a Light Railway Order.

Several residents were against the idea, and a public inquiry listened to objections that trams would create unacceptable noise and harm the natural beauty of the Axe valley, but the town council argued that the tramway would become a major asset to the area, and after assurances were given about safety at Colyford level crossing, Claude won the day.

The new line would be built to a gauge of 2ft 9ins. Already in 1969, Claude had built Car 8 to larger proportions than its predecessors in readiness for the wider track.

From September 1969, the complete Eastbourne system had to be dismantled, transported 100 miles westwards and reassembled before the 1970 holiday season ended. Claude and his assistant Allan Gardner made 36 return lorry journeys between Eastbourne and Seaton.

On 28 August 1970, Car 8 became the first tram to run in passenger service on the Seaton branch, taking power from a battery car as overhead wires had yet to be installed. A depot at Riverside just north of the original Seaton branch station, which was demolished following closure, was installed so that winter the existing trams could be regauged.

The line reached Colyford, the midway point, but before the first full season could start, Claude died from a heart attack on 2 April 1971.

Allan Gardner took over as managing director to complete the project with the

The handle does it all! SEATON TRAMWAY

aid of volunteers. A 'train' returned to the Seaton branch in the shape of a diesel shunter boughtto assist works Car 02 in hauling equipment.

Passing loops were installed at Axmouth and Swan's Nest, allowing trams to operate simultaneously. During 1973 overhead wire and fittings were installed, and the first tram powered from the overhead lines ran that September.

To make a success of the line, a town centre presence was urgently needed, and land was bought to lay a new trackbed to a fresh terminus site next to Harbour Road car park, the work being finished in May 1975.

Flood damage in 1978 and subsequent remedial work delayed the final extension to Colyton until 1980.

Attention then switched to expanding the fleet. Former Metropolitan Tramways Car 94, obtained by Claude in 1962, was reduced in size by cutting the body length ways in half and narrowing it by 2ft. It entered service in 1984 as enclosed single-deck saloon Car 14, launched into traffic by the late comedian Larry Grayson.

Likewise, original Bournemouth Tramways Car 106 was reduced in scale and re-emerged from the workshops in 1992 as Car 16.

Colyton

Colyford

Seaton

Manx Electric Railway-style 'toastrack' Car 17. ROBIN JONES

In 1998, former Exeter Tramways Car 19, which ran in the city from 1906 until the system closed in 1931, was reduced in size and restored from derelict condition to become the third enclosed saloon,

More new trams followed in the 21st century in the form of Cars 9, 10 and 11, all of a hybrid design based on the old Plymouth and Blackburn full-size versions.

In short, each tram is a unique miniature masterpiece. The tramway now has extraordinary varieties of vehicle from open double-deckers and basic wooden seats to luxuriously upholstered wood-panelled cars.

There are enough trams to run a service every few minutes in the high season.

Today, the tramway carries more than 100,000 visitors a year, numbers that compare favourably with the patronage of the old steam branch. ∎

The luxurious interior of Car 14, built from the cut-down body of Metropolitan Electric Tramways Car 94. ROBIN JONES

The complete Rich Morris monorail network at Blaenau Ffestiniog. JOHN STRETTON

The steam monorail

Blaenau Ffestiniog is not just the upper terminus of the Ffestiniog Railway. It is also the home of the world's only steam monorail 0-2-0 locomotive, which runs on a private system where the term rail (singular) way means exactly that!

It was on Sunday 13 December 1997 that a small steam locomotive with one very big difference made its maiden run over a short length of track at Sunbury-on-Thames in Middlesex.

From the chassis upwards it looked every bit a typical narrow gauge tank engine, a bit like a 'quarry Hunslet' 0-4-0 saddle tank, resplendent in its bright blue livery.

However, there was something about the wheels. It had just two of them!

What was believed to be the world's only 0-2-0 tank engine had been built to run on a monorail.

Dubbed the 'Monoloco', its successful debut was the culmination of a 25-year dream by enthusiast Rich Morris, who previously owned the Gloddfa Ganol narrow gauge railway and mining centre at Blaenau Ffestiniog which closed in 1997.

The Monoloco had taken shape over two years far from Snowdonia, having been built by engineering company Century Millwrights on Platts Eyot, a small island in the River Thames.

Rich, who had been collecting monorail equipment for 30 years, had drawn up rough sketches of his dream project and given them to project engineer John Vineer, who made several adjustments to make the Monoloco a 'goer'.

Standing 6ft high and 11ft long, the locomotive was constructed on the chassis of a Metalair Ltd wagon from an industrial monorail line used by Bovis at Westbury. Rich had acquired the manufacturing rights of Metalair Ltd of Wokingham, Britain's only commercial monorail builder, in 1983.

The Monoloco, which made its public debut at the International Model Railway Exhibition at Kensington Olympia in December 1997, runs on driving wheels with double flanges which straddle a triangular section running rail that is one inch wide at the top of the rail.

Outriding stabiliser wheels at the front and back ride on the 3in bottom section of the rail, to keep the Monoloco steady.

The height of the track can be altered from 14in above ground level, to a maximum 7ft 8in, using stands of different sizes. The system was originally built in the 1940s by Road Machines (Drayton) Ltd of West Drayton, Middlesex, which produced internal combustion and diesel-powered monorail equipment for use on building sites – a version of the traditional contractor's temporary railway.

The Monoloco and other monorail vehicles built by Rich now operate on his private site which is occasionally opened for arranged enthusiast parties.

The steam monorail concept is probably best-known in Britain for the Listowel & Ballybunion Railway, but that was by no means the earliest example.

With monorails, as with the steam locomotive, Britain can claim a world first. The Cheshunt Railway, which was completed in 1825 and worked by a horse, was the first to carry passengers, as it did at its opening, although it was designed by Henry Robinson Palmer to carry bricks .

In 1876, General Le-Roy Stone first demonstrated a steam-driven monorail at the United States Centennial Exposition in Philadelphia in 1876. It comprised a double-decker vehicle with two main wheels, the rear one driven by a rotary steam engine.

A modified version of General Stone's Centennial monorail was employed on a four-mile line between Bradford and Gilmore in Pennsylvania built to transport oil drilling equipment and personnel to Derrick City. Local residents also began using it.

The worst disaster in monorail history took place on 27 January 1879 when a new and more powerful engine coupled to a flat car full of officials was run at high speed to show what it was capable of doing. The boiler exploded and the train crashed into a creek, killing the

One of a kind: the 0-2-0 steam Monoloco in action at its owner's private site in Blaenau Ffestiniog on 22 August 2009. JOHN STRETTON

driver, fireman and three passengers, leaving the rest severely injured. The monorail was abandoned soon afterwards.

Probably the oldest and crudest monorail still operable is at the Indian Railway Museum in Delhi, Unlike later systems where the rolling stock straddles and balances on the railhead the Patiala State monorail had conventional rolling stock with the second rail replaced by a flat track on which a cartwheel rolled, stopping the whole ensemble from toppling over, like the stabiliser on a child's bicycle.

The locomotive was, uniquely, an 0-3-0 with double flanged driving wheels.

The system was built in 1909 and closed in 1927, following which the engine and stock were stored and forgotten until rediscovered and restored in the 1970s to run at the museum. ∎

Modern traction not steam hauls this train on the Blaenau monorail! JOHN STRETTON

Narrow gauge locomotives like this Ruston diesel engine, which dates from 1936, were used for moving ammunition through the underground complex. It is pictured on site in 2002. M HESKETH-ROBERTS/ENGLISH HERITAGE

From Brunel to the Bomb!

In certain railway enthusiast circles, for many years there persisted a Cold War theory that after the end of steam, large quantities of redundant locomotives were squirreled away by stealth and hidden in a vast bunker in the south of England, a strategic reserve lying in readiness for a time of international crisis or global conflict, when diesel fuel would be in short supply.

The sad truth was that there was no secret hoard of steam engines; however, there certainly was an underground railway leading off the GWR main line into a secret underground city which would have become Britain's emergency seat of government the event of a nuclear war.

Words by Keith Falconer of English Heritage and Robin Jones.

Bath stone quarried from Corsham has provided the raw material for magnificent buildings around the world. While quarrying was taking place around the Wiltshire town in the 18th century, it took off big time when Isambard Kingdom Brunel and an army of 4000 navvies arrived in 1841 to bore his stupendous Box Tunnel – and inadvertently stumbled on rich seams of freestone.

The chance discovery led to a stone mining boom, with more than 1000 people employed in the mines by the end of the 19th century, and the railway facilitating the export of the stone across the country and beyond. Huge underground caverns appeared as the seams were exploited, and a spur off the GWR main line at the eastern portal of Box Tunnel disappeared into a passageway of its own to take the stone out.

The quarrying was almost brought to an end with emergence of cheaper building materials in the 1920s, leaving many miles of underground stone workings redundant.

However, another use was found for the mines…

This turntable is sited in the underground locomotive workshop. M HESKETH-ROBERTS/ENGLISH HERITAGE

The underground station in military use, with standard gauge box vans lined up alongside. CORSHAM HERITAGE CENTRE

The eastern portal of Box Tunnel in GWR days, with the freight line leading into the quarries on the right. Initially it was big enough only to take wagons, but was enlarged in the 30s to accept early main line diesel shunters, chosen because they would not emit sparks in the ammunition dump. CORSHAM HERITAGE CENTRE

The idea of bombproof shelters to protect men and stores is enshrined in much of military defence planning since the advent of military explosives. However, it was only with the threat of aerial bombardment that it was to escape the confines of designed fortresses.

Thus, immediately prior to World War One with the apparent threat of Zeppelin raids, the Ministry of Munitions sought to protect stockpiles of bulk high explosives by storing them underground.

Initially, existing mines and caves were utilised such as a salt mine near Northwich in Cheshire adapted to house 1500 tons of explosives for north country filling factories and the Chislehurst caves near Bromley for the Woolwich Arsenal.

Likewise, a small Bathstone mine at The Ridge near Corsham was converted in 1915 for the storage of TNT and cordite. The development of underground

munitions depots in the inter-war years is marked by indecision on behalf of government ministries and inter-service rivalry and argument, but in 1934 when rearmament was once again on the agenda following Hitler's accession as Chancellor of Germany the process gained some momentum. In the summer of 1936, the War Office, having decided that the stone mines in the Corsham area was the preferred location for its main underground ammunition depot, completed the purchase of Ridge, Tunnel and Eastlays quarries at a cost of £47,000. From these rather modest beginnings was to develop the Central Ammunition Depot, Corsham which, by

1943, encompassed some 125 acres of subterranean chambers containing 300,000 tons of explosives and munitions.

Its widely dispersed components stretched from Limpley Stoke and Monkton Farleigh (one of the largest single quarries) in the west and Westwood and Bradford-on-Avon in the south to Corsham and Gastard in the north and east.

The total cost of the depot was over £4,500,000 – a far cry from the initial estimated requirement for six acres at a cost of £100,000 originally envisaged.

As already mentioned, the 50-acre Tunnel Quarry was directly served by a standard gauge branch off the main line. ➤

'The quarrying was almost brought to an end with emergence of cheaper building materials in the 1920s'

This branch was upgraded for military use. Complete with a 750ft underground platform and refuge sidings, it ran for around 2000ft underground, to which 1800ft of refuge sidings can be added.

The standard gauge line was worked by three Hunslet 0-6-0 diesel shunters from the reception sidings three miles to the east at the GWR's Thingley Junction where there were a few temporary buildings.

Daily maintenance of the locomotives was conducted at the underground locomotive shed but major overhauls were undertaken at MoD Bicester. The standard gauge line fed a 2ft gauge railway system with diesel locomotives, turntables, engine houses and workshops serving the underground ammunition 'districts'.

The narrow gauge system was installed from the beginning on temporary tracks and was used mainly for very heavy ammunition items, as the extensive conveyor belt system in the complex was much preferred, as it has separate receipt and dispatch belts. Efforts were made to maintain an air of secrecy about the works going on at Corsham. By way of subterfuge, rumours were circulated that the Ministry of Food was building an emergency food dump there.

At the onset of World War Two, RAF command centres were, whenever possible, located underground and in the case of No 10 Fighter Command covering the West Country this was accomplished in Browns Quarry – a spur off Tunnel Quarry.

The onslaught of the German air offensive in 1940 also caused the various supply ministries to seek protected sites for crucial industries such as the manufacture of aircraft engines and weapons (and even for the storage of national treasures from the British Museum, the Victoria & Albert Museum, the Banqueting House and Westminster Abbey).

Huge sums were spent constructing underground factories in new tunnels driven into hillsides such as at Drakelow near Kidderminster and converting existing quarries as at Henley-on-Thames, Westwood near Bradford-on-Avon… and at Corsham itself.   Under pressure from Lord Beaverbrook, the vast Spring Quarry, on the other side of Box Tunnel from Tunnel Quarry, was requisitioned late in 1940 and was converted by Ministry of Air Production for factory use at exorbitant cost to become 'the largest underground factory in the world'.

It was to be occupied by the Bristol Aircraft Company for the production of Centaurus engines while a separate part was occupied by BSA for the manufacture of gun barrels (including half of the country's entire output of Hispano and Polsen barrels).

When Spring Quarry was in BAC occupancy, the BAC chairman, Sir Reginald Verdon Smith, commissioned a professional artist, Olga Lehmann, to decorate some of the canteen areas with vivid floor-to-ceiling murals.

Over 40 of these survive in one of the canteen areas despite 60 years of disregard and neglect.

They are executed in a distinctive style very much of the pre-war period and mainly depict racing and attendant showground themes interspersed with drinking scenes, cricket matches and even missionary boiling!

The expenditure on the underground depots was to be justified after the war by their continued use as ammunition and naval stores for 50 years but the factories, as such, were an expensive fiasco.

By the time they finally opened early in 1943, German bombing was no longer the

Shells being stacked inside the depot.
CORSHAM HERITAGE CENTRE

The shelves of the underground city are still stacked with supplies for worst case scenarios. M HESKETH-ROBERTS/ENGLISH HERITAGE

The Central Ammunition Depot was equipped with its own locomotive workshop and inspection pit.
M HESKETH-ROBERTS/ENGLISH HERITAGE

Munitions were transported into and out of the depot by rail. At the main platform, they were loaded onto a conveyor belt for distribution within the site. This is the platform pictured in 2002. When we saw an underground railway station in the Torchwood headquarters in the BBC TV Dr Who spin-off, we all knew it was nonsense, didn't we? M HESKETH-ROBERTS/ENGLISH HERITAGE

threat that it had been when they were first conceived and they were less than satisfactory for their purpose. When they closed just two years later, the bill for their construction had exceeded £20-million.

For the next half-century, however, the whole suite of converted Corsham quarries achieved a valuable second life as home to a variety of Cold War uses whose chronology reflects the course of strategic thinking throughout this period.

Codenamed originally SUBTERFUGE this facility developed in the early 60s under the codenames BURLINGTON (and finally TURNSTILE) into an office for Prime Minister Harold Macmillan, the War Cabinet and Chiefs of Staff, and possibly the Royal Family. It was said that it could safely house up to 4000 central Government personnel in the event of a

nuclear strike, in complete isolation from the outside world, for up to three months.

Having more than 60 miles of internal roads and covering 35 acres 100ft below Corsham, the Barracks Hill military underground site was designed not only to accommodate the then Conservative Prime Minister, Harold MacMillan, but the entire Cabinet Office, civil servants and an army of domestic support staff.

The New York grid-style city of roads and avenues was equipped with all the facilities needed to survive – underground hospitals, laboratories canteens, kitchens and laundries to storerooms of supplies, accommodation areas, offices and a bar.

An underground lake and treatment plant could provide all the drinking water needed while 12 huge tanks could store the fuel required to keep the four massive

generators, in the underground power station, running for up to three months. Air could also be kept at a constant humidity and heated to around 20C.

The city also had the second largest telephone exchange in Britain, a BBC studio from which the Prime Minister could address the nation and an internal Lamson Tube system that could send messages using compressed air throughout the complex.

The site was so top secret that many of the civil servants, who had been allocated a desk at Burlington, had no knowledge of it.

The Emergency Government War Headquarters had its final upgrading in the early years of the Thatcher government but with the end of the Cold War in the early 1990s these uses have been scaled down or abandoned. ➤

Rail tunnels diverge inside the depot. M HESKETH-ROBERTS/ENGLISH HERITAGE

The underground depot continued in use during the Cold War; this kitchen area dates from the final phase of use. M HESKETH-ROBERTS/ENGLISH HERITAGE

By 1943, the Central Ammunition Depot was the largest in the world. Munitions were transported on these 2ft gauge railway wagons, of which several survive underground. M HESKETH-ROBERTS/ENGLISH HERITAGE

The original raison d'etre for the military presence has long since gone – the last munitions were shipped out or destroyed by the end of 1962 and the stores function was finally wound down in the 1990s.

In December 2008, with the underground reservoir drained, emptied of fuel and supplies and with a token staff of just four, the site was finally decommissioned. Much of the complex has now been mothballed or sold, parts of it being used for commercial storage, though there is still a significant RAF and military communications presence.

Among the decaying evidence of disused offices and stores are poignant and sinister reminders of this fascinating but little heralded chapter in our history, such as shelving with signs GAS, BIO and ATOM. The little 2ft gauge Hunslet four-wheeled diesel which operated on the system, WD1, is still underground.

The proposed development of the site by its present occupant – Defence Communication Services Agency – has involved English Heritage in photographic recording of some of the remains and advising on the management of both the surface and underground structures.

There is the argument that, just like a medieval castle or Roman camp, it is now part of the nation's history and should be preserved, at least in part. However, much of it is deteriorating due to damp and its future appears to be rather bleak. Yet if at least part of it could be saved and maybe opened to the public, what a fascinating heritage railway the internal system would make!

Sadly, it never did contain a stock of former GWR and British Railways steam locomotives despite the enthusiast conspiracy theories that abounded about them being smuggled away under cover of darkness and their numbers never appearing in the records of scrap merchants as a result. We must now accept that they were cut up at the end of the steam age and lost forever.

The entrance tunnel is now bricked up. That did not stop three men entering Box Tunnel in September 2003 looking for it, and ending up in court after causing six-hour delays to main line services while they were rescued. ■

The rail tunnel leading into the underground depot was closed off in 1974. This view was taken in the mid-90s. CORSHAM HERITAGE CENTRE

A Cold War era view of the 'overground' railway at Corsham: in the early 1960s, a Western Region diesel hydraulic passes a GWR pannier tank at Corsham signalbox. None of the passengers would have been aware of the colossal underground city nearby.
CORSHAM HERITAGE CENTRE

The widest narrow gauge

Two classic Peckett saddle tanks forming the entire locomotive fleet of the Lee Moor Tramway are preserved, and they could probably be restored to running order for a reasonable cost. Yet it is unlikely to happen – for there is now no railway on which they could be run – all because of two-and-a-half inches. This unusual and historically complex line was built to the 'Dartmoor gauge' of 4ft 6in – whereas the national network is 4ft 8½in standard gauge.

Lee Moor No 1 at the Wheal Martyn China Clay Museum near St Austell. ROBSUE888 - FLICKR.COM

The Lee Moor Tramway is probably best known among enthusiasts for its flat crossing of the GWR's London-Penance four-track main line at Laira Junction near Plymouth. Into the second half of the 20th century, with the aid of wooden boards between the rails, horses would haul short rakes of laden china clay wagons across the tracks which were the domain of Kings, Castles and other illustrious express passenger locomotives.

Such an anachronism which lasted into the early years of the diesel era would easily justify the tramway a place in this book on its own. However, it is here because it utilised the widest narrow gauge of all.

The use of 4ft 6in gauge track dates back to the days before there was serious talk about a national railway network. ➤

Above: **Lee Moor Crossing on the GWR Launceston branch in 1922.** FHC CASBOURN /STEPHENSON LOCOMOTIVE SOCIETY
Right: *Lee Moor No 2* hauling 17 empty wagons towards Torycombe level crossing on 18 August 1939. ER SHPHERD

Indeed, there was no real reason why , who built Prince's Town in the heart of the Dartmoor and named it after the Prince of Wales, later King George IV, should have chosen one particular gauge over another when he planned his horse-worked Plymouth and Dartmoor Railway as a means to open up the moor to habitation.

It was Tyrwhitt who had earlier suggested to the Admiralty that his town could be the base of a prisoner-of-war camp to house captured Napoleonic militiamen, and so Dartmoor Prison was completed in 1809. When peace was declared in 1815, the prison was left empty, and Tyrwhitt looked to rail as a means of reclaiming the moor as farmland and transporting granite from local quarries.

The first large-scale railway in Plymouth, the 25-mile line from the city's Sutton Pool harbour to Princetown opened on 26 September 1823. Its 4ft 6in gauge henceforth became known as 'Dartmoor gauge'

In 1883 the top section of the railway above Yelverton became converted to standard gauge as the , later part of the GWR empire.

Tywrwhitt's railway fell into disuse around 1900, and most of the track had been lifted by 1916.

The Lee Moor Tramway was a privately owned mineral railway that was built to carry china clay and other produce from southern Dartmoor to the quays at Plymouth, and used the track for the lower portion of its journey. It was likewise built to Dartmoor gauge.

Lord Morley, who owned the mineral rights at Lee Moor, where rich deposits of china clay had been identified, leased them to J&W Phillips in September 1833. Several schemes to build a railway linking the harbour to Lee Moor were built, work on the successful one beginning in 1853. However, it was poorly built and in June 1856 Lord Morley and Phillips secured the right to run their own china clay traffic to

Plymouth – as long as the 4ft 6in gauge remained – and rebuilt the tramway, including the viaduct at Wotter and the great incline at Torycombe. Five years earlier, the South Devon Railway had bought the 's Sutton Harbour branch and converted it to dual gauge, Brunel's 7ft 0¼in encompassing the existing 4ft 6in.

The Torycombe incline was ceremoniously reopened on 24 September 1858 by the Earl and Countess of Morley and marked the official opening date of the Lee Moor Tramway.

Until 1899 the tramway was operated by horses, but two 0-4-0 saddle tanks were ordered from Peckett of Bristol to handle the increase in clay production. The line

was upgraded to accommodate them and an engine shed was constructed at Torycombe clay works.

Lee Moor No 1 and Lee Moor No 2 were the only 4ft 6in gauge locomotives ever built by Peckett. Their livery was green with yellow and green lining and dull red frames and wheels. They operated only on the northern section above the one-and-a-quarter-mile long 1-in-11 rope-worked Cann incline; below there, the rest of the tramway to the harbour including the famous flat crossing was worked by horses until the end.

Closure of the tramway began in 1910 when the top part of the line from Lee Moor village to Cholwich Town pits was shut down. Torycombe incline closed in

Andrew Barclay 0-4-0ST *Albert* on the Plym Valley Railway's newly finished Lee Moor Crossing. A cyclepath now follows the route of the tramway, below which a pipeline to carry china clay is buried. DAVID ELBROW/PVR

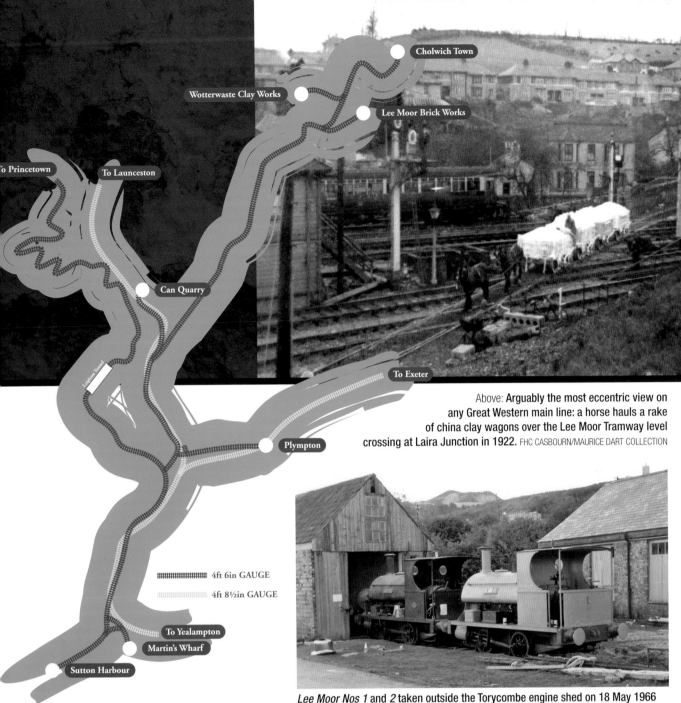

Above: **Arguably the most eccentric view on any Great Western main line: a horse hauls a rake of china clay wagons over the Lee Moor Tramway level crossing at Laira Junction in 1922.** FHC CASBOURN/MAURICE DART COLLECTION

Map labels:
- Cholwich Town
- Wotterwaste Clay Works
- Lee Moor Brick Works
- To Princetown
- To Launceston
- Can Quarry
- Leigham Tunnel
- To Exeter
- Plympton
- 4ft 6in GAUGE
- 4ft 8½in GAUGE
- To Yealampton
- Martin's Wharf
- Sutton Harbour

Lee Moor Nos 1 and *2* taken outside the Torycombe engine shed on 18 May 1966 for the first time in more than 20 years. ER SHEPHERD

1936, having been kept open until then to transport goods for the village and stone from the local quarry.

The rest of the line was closed shortly after the start of World War Two but was reopened to transport naval stores that had been moved from the heavily bombed to Lee Moor village for safekeeping.

The tramway reopened properly on 8 October 1945 but closed again in 1947, leaving only the section from Marsh Mills to Maddocks Concrete Works at Laira, along which sand was conveyed in order to maintain the right-of-way across the at Laira Junction.

This crossing was used 14 times in 1958 but it dropped to six in 1959 and only four in 1960. The final crossing was made on 26 August 1960, at 11.19am on the outward journey and finally at 1.27pm when the horse and empty tracks returned towards Marsh Mills.

The tramway was then dismantled and replaced with a pipeline above Marsh Mills, although the track remained between Marsh Mills and Laira. Today, a cyclepath follows much of the moorland route of the tramway.

The Lee Moor Preservation Society, an offshoot of the Plymouth Railway Circle, was formed in February 1964 to carry out work on the two steam locomotives. Lee Moor No 2 was cosmetically restored for display in the National Trust's Saltram House at Plympton to where it was moved on 20 July 1970. Lee Moor No 1 went to the Wheal Martyn China Clay Museum near St Austell on 17 March 1975, by which time the society had been disbanded and absorbed back into the circle from which it originated in the first place.

In 2001, Lee Moor No 2 was transferred to the custody of the South Devon Railway at Buckfastleigh, where it is safely kept in a shed, together with the last surviving Lee

Moor Tramway china clay wagon. Agreement was also reached for its sister engine to follow at a later date.

The original thinking was for one of them to be returned to steam so it could run on a short demonstration line – but where is the revenue-earning potential in such a venture for a heritage railway, like all others, forever running on a tight budget? To the untrained eye, it looks like a classic standard gauge Peckett industrial saddle tank, of which many survive in preservation, so where is the 'wow' factor for the general public. Regauging it to standard gauge would destroy its historical appeal. Therein lies a preservation enigma.

In 2009, steam returned to a small part of the Lee Moors Tramway. The Plym Valley Railway, a standard gauge heritage line at Marsh Mills which has been laid on part of the GWR Plymouth-Yelverton-Launceston route, now runs as far as the flat crossing which took the tramway across it. ∎

Sail away!

Looking down the railway to Spurn Point from the top of the lighthouse. On the right are the lifeboat crew's cottages.
KE HARTLEY COLLECTION/RON REDMAN

While the steam engine technology of the first railway locomotives was also applied to ships, could the principles of sail in turn be applied to railway traction? Bizarrely enough, that did happen, in several places around Britain, perhaps the best-known being the Spurn Head Railway.

Spurn Head, the great sandspit across the mouth of the Humber.

Spurn Head is the name given to the distinctive narrow sand spit that reaches across the mouth of the River Humber from its northern bank as it enters the North Sea.

Comprising of sand and shingle eroded from the Holderness coastline and washed down from as far away as Flamborough Head, it stretches for over three miles into the estuary, but is as little as 50 yards wide in places.

At the rounded tip is a lifeboat station which was built in 1810 – houses for the crew and their families being added later – and a disused lighthouse. Since 1960, Spurn head has been owned by the Yorkshire Wildlife Trust and is a designated National Nature Reserve, Heritage Coast and is part of the Humber Flats, Marshes and Coast Special Protection Area.

At one time, it also had its own railway.

With the onset of World War One and the perceived threat of German forces to the east coast and the ports of Hull, Grimsby, Immingham and Killingholme, then newly established as an oil terminal, the War Department regarded it as imperative to fortify Spurn Head and the entrance to the Humber.

The lifeboatmen's sail bogie in use on the Spurn Head Railway. KE HARTLEY COLLECTION/RON REDMAN

Visitors enjoy a ride on a Spurn Head 'land ship.' KE HARTLEY COLLECTION/RON REDMAN

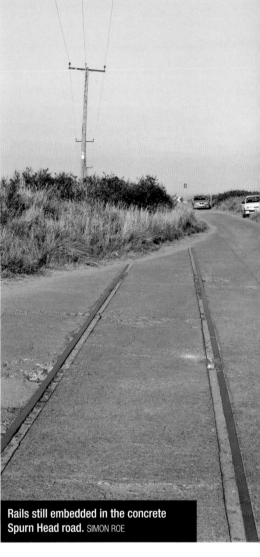

Rails still embedded in the concrete Spurn Head road. SIMON ROE

Two massive island-like forts in the estuary itself were built, Haile Sand Fort which lies on the low water mark between Cleethorpes and Humberston on the Lincolnshire coast, and Bull Fort rests on a sandbank in the middle of the river.

Bull Fort was built with great difficulty as the sandbank on which it rests is 11ft below low water.

It was constructed to a circular design on interlocking steel piles in the form of caissons. The upper part of the fort is up to 50ft above high water and comprises three floors and a basement floor, with an outer wall of concrete faced with 12in thick armour plating.

It accommodated a garrison of 200 men and provided all necessary facilities.

On Spurn Head, two coastal artillery 9.2in batteries were added at either end of Spurn Head, with 4in and 4.7in quick-firing guns in between.

Much of the materials for the building work was brought in by water, but the War Department decided to add its own railway to bring both men and materials to the new fortress at Spurn Head. Before the railway came, access to Spurn Head by land involved a three-mile walk over sand dunes.

Contractor CJ Wills of Manchester and London was engaged and brought five tank engines to build the line, one staying on afterwards to operate it.

The track comprises second-hand bullhead rail laid on cast-iron chairs obtained from the Great Central Railway, with many of the chairs carrying the initials MS&LR, the company's pre-1899 name of the Manchester, Sheffield and Lincolnshire Railway. The standard gauge line ran from a northern terminus at Kilnsea, at a fort named Godwin Battery, for three-and-three-quarter miles to Green Battery at Spurn Point, where a two-track stone engine shed was built just north of the lighthouse. The contractors also built a railway pier near the tip of Spurn Head, complete with steam crane, to receive materials brought in by river.

The small fleet of rolling stock comprised a coach built for the North London Railway; it was said have had a murder committed in it before it was moved to Yorkshire. Its body was later privately bought and moved to the grounds of a bungalow at Kilnsea. There were at first also two open wagons.

One of three Hudswell Clarke 0-4-0 saddle tanks used to build the line, No 402 of 1893 *Lord Mayor*, survived into

preservation, and is now part of the Vintage Carriages Trust collection at the Museum of Rail Travel at Ingrow on the Keighley & Worth Valley Railway elsewhere in Yorkshire.

Another contractor's locomotive was Kenyon, a Vulcan Foundry inside-cylinder saddle tank dating from 1888 and acquired by the War Department in 1916, staying on to provide traction until 1929, after it had been run into the ground. It was scrapped at the Kilnsea sidings shortly afterwards.

Several petrol-engined railcars, all but one made by Drewery, appeared from 1920 onwards when a 12-seater, works number 1119, was delivered. In 1929, a bigger and more powerful Hardy railcar was obtained, but it suffered a cracked cylinder block and radiator in the icy winter of 1940 and afterwards was used as a locomotive-hauled coach, being scrapped in 1947.

A Hudswell Clarke railcar which arrived in June 1933 ended its day at Bicester Royal Engineers' depot as a runner truck in the early 1970s.

Another form of traction which saw service on the line was an adapted Itala racing car! Fitted with flanged wheels, it was said to be capable of reaching 60mph on the line. It survived until at least 1940. ➤

However, the railway's most unusual and unforgettable feature was the use of two sail bogies or trolleys which emerged during or after World War One.

They were basic wooden platforms with flanged wheels, similar to the type once commonly used by platelayers, but with a mast fixed in the centre, to which a large balanced lug sail was fixed and braced to the corners of the trolley.

They were built and used by the lifeboatmen and the men working for the War Department, who often gave trips on them to visitors. No seats were provided and passengers had to sit directly on the decking.

The sail bogies had no proper method of braking and they were usually stopped by dropping a heavy piece of timber in front of the wheels.

The Great Northern Railway had made much of the fact that Skegness was so bracing in its Jolly Fisherman poster, in a bid to encourage people to visit the resort by train, and yet here further up the east coast was a railway which powered itself by the same gusts! An early form of 'green' transport, they were by far the cheapest forms of traction on the line both to build and to run!

It is said that the sail bogies could reach a reasonable speed, but too much wind and they would blow over. On calmer days, the sail bogie had to be pushed by hand.

Nevertheless, they proved a popular alternative to having to walk all the way to and from Kilnsea.

The military sail bogie was often used to check that the line was clear of sand, which frequently drifted over the tracks.

The earliest recorded use of a trolley by the lifeboatmen was during 1915.

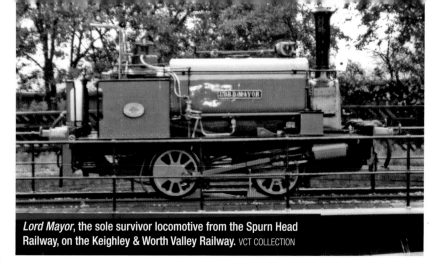

Lord Mayor, the sole survivor locomotive from the Spurn Head Railway, on the Keighley & Worth Valley Railway. VCT COLLECTION

Vulcan saddle tank No 1233 of 1888 Kenyon hauling a Spurn Head Railway train. KE HARTLEY COLLECTION/RON REDMAN

There were, of course, accidents and scrapes. On one occasion, a group of soldiers who had been drinking at the Blue Bell Inn in Kilnsea boarded the trolley, hoisted the sail, and set off for Spurn Point. They all fell asleep while in transit, at the same time the wind picked up.

Hurling towards the southern terminus, one of the soldiers woke up in time to stop the sail bogie ramming the battery entrance gates.

Another instance saw a sail bogie sent to Kilnsea to collect a married couple. It rapidly gathered speed on the way back and when it reached 40mph the inexperienced man in charge panicked and jumped off. The husband followed him, but his wife stayed on the trolley, and sustained cuts to her face, while the wind dropped and the sail bogie slowed down before the fort was reached.

The Reverend Alfred Poulsom, who served as Methodist chaplain at Spurn Point, wrote that on one occasion a sail bogie powered towards a coastguard walking on the track not only with his back to the oncoming 'land ship' but completely oblivious to it. The sail was lowered to no effect, and then the 'brake' was dropped in front of the sail bogie, which cut through it without stopping. Luckily, the coastguard saw the danger at the last minute and jumped clear with just seconds to spare.

The military sail bogie was later fitted with a Raleigh 350cc side valve engine and gearbox, but it was wrecked on its trial run when it ended up under a railway truck due to wrongly set points.

It seems that sail power was last used on the railway during the Second World War, or just afterwards.

Steam returned to the railway in early 1940, when the strategic importance of Spurn Head was again realised and a London & North Eastern Railway Y8 class 0-4-0, No 559, was sent from Hull (Dairycoates) depot to Patrington station in 1940. There it was placed on a low-loader behind an LNER Scammel truck and taken to Kilnsea, where it was re-railed, and nicknamed 'Black Sapper'. The rolling stock fleet was increased by three box vans and three open wagons, at least one of which was converted to carry a gun.

During the Second World War, work on building a concrete road to Spurn Point was started, with the help of the railway that it would supersede. At the time, the railway carried much Royal Engineers traffic during work to fortify the sea defences and prevent the spit from being breached.

The railway was declared redundant in the winter of 1951-52. Contractor Thomas W Ward Ltd of Sheffield dismantled the line. The War Department decommissioned the Spurn Head military establishments between 1956-59.

The engine sheds in 1952, when the line was dismantled. KE HARTLEY COLLECTION/RON REDMAN

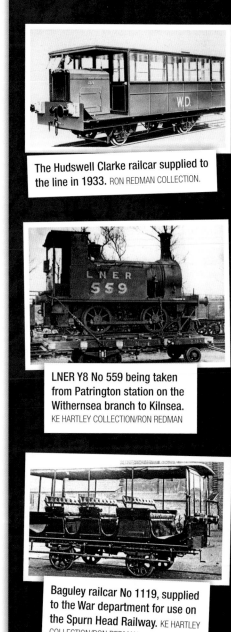

The Hudswell Clarke railcar supplied to the line in 1933. RON REDMAN COLLECTION.

LNER Y8 No 559 being taken from Patrington station on the Withernsea branch to Kilnsea. KE HARTLEY COLLECTION/RON REDMAN

Baguley railcar No 1119, supplied to the War department for use on the Spurn Head Railway. KE HARTLEY COLLECTION/RON REDMAN

The engine shed and workshop, and adjacent fuel and water buildings were unfortunately removed by troops in a demolition exercise between August 1966 and April 1967.

There are still traces of the line to be seen today: at three points, rails are still embedded in the concrete road which exists and a short section of track remains inside what was the entrance to the Spurn battery.

The railway pier was gradually dismantled in the 1970s and now only a few rotting timbers remain.

Spurn Head was not the only place where sail power was used.

The Francis Alpha cement works at Cliffe on the Isle of Grain in Kent works had a railway linking it to a quay a mile away. After the Alpha works closed in the 50s, a sail-powered trolley was used on the line to inspect the sea defences. A sail trolley was built by Ransomes & Rapier at its

Kilnsea

Lighthouse

Spurn Head

Waterside Works in Ipswich in 1869. A sail bogie ran on a railway at South Gare, Teeside and one existed on the military line between Fort Blockhouse and Fort Monckton in Gosport around 1895.

The Admiralty Wireless Tramway at Port Stanley in the Falkland Islands had several sail trolleys in the early 20th century.

The Spooner family who developed the Festiniog Railway in the 19th century built their own inspection trolley in the shape of a boat complete with sail, although, like many slate trains on the line, it was gravity powered. It came to grief when it crashed into a train.

A replica was built and made its appearance at the line's annual vintage weekend in 2005. ■

Steam and seed oil

One of the biggest names in British locomotive building was – and still is – Hunslet, whose renowned products were exported across the globe. At home, they had the last word in steam, building both the final standard and narrow gauge engines of the steam age in Britain. Unlike its long-vanished rivals, the firm is still building steam, for the heritage era; not in a Leeds suburb, but on a farm in Staffordshire, where a magnificent private multi-gauge railway has been developed.

In 1864, civil engineering contractor John Towlerton Leather founded a locomotive-building company in Jack Lane, Hunslet, Leeds, and named it Hunslet after the locality. The first engine to be built was *Linden*, a standard gauge 0-6-0 saddle tank delivered to railway civil engineering contractor Brassey and Ballard in 1865. Six years later, his works manager, James Campbell, bought the company for £25,000.

In Britain, the firm was hugely successful in building locomotives for industry, notably the 0-4-0 saddle tanks for the North Wales slate mines, which became known as 'quarry Hunslets'. The first, Dinorwic, was a 1ft 10¾in gauge locomotive for the Dinorwic Slate Quarry at Llanberis. This engine, later renamed Charlie, was the first of 20 similar engines built for this quarry and did much to establish Hunslet as a major builder of quarry engines.

The first Hunslet engine built for export was the firm's No 10, an 0-4-0 saddle tank exported to Java. By 1902, Hunslet had supplied engines worldwide.

The firm also built main line locomotives, including, after World War One, 90 Fowler 'Jinty' 3F 0-6-0 tank engines for the London, Midland & Scottish Railway.

Several other builders were bust during the depression, including Avonside, Manning Wardle, Kitson and Kerr Stuart, and Hunslet acquired the rights to their patterns and designs.

In the 1930s, Hunslet worked on the development of the diesel locomotive, and this continued during World War Two. A key post-war produce was the Hunslet flameproof diesel engine for use in the coal mines. Diesels accounted for more and more of the business from the late 40s onwards. The other type of steam locomotive produced in vast numbers by the firm, and other builders under licence, was the 55050 class of 0-6-0 saddle tanks, or Hunslet 'Austerity', which appeared in 1942 and eventually numbered 484 examples. The class became the standard British shunting locomotive during World War Two, when 337 were sold to the War Department, 75 subsequently being sold on to the London & North Eastern Railway, where

Britain's last standard gauge new steam locomotive (of the steam age rather than preservation era) appeared in the form of Hunslet Austerity 0-6-0ST No 3890. BOB FRISE/BRC

Hunslet celebrated building steam locomotives in a third century when 0-4-0 saddle tanks *Jack Lane* and *Statfold* were outshopped. The pair are seen together at the Statford Barn Railway. BRIAN SHARPE

Right: *Trangkil No 4* heads a passenger train along the Field Railway. SBR

Below: *Sid*, a new compressed air mines locomotive, being driven by its builder, Statfold volunteer Roy Etherington of Tamworth, who built it in the railway's workshops. The design is based on a Lishman & Young original, which worked mines in Durham from 1878 for 20 years; the tub it is pulling is a genuine one from New Lount Colliery. While other countries like the USA persevered with the development of compressed air locomotives until diesel and battery electric alternatives had been invented, Britain gave up on the concept around 1900. SBR

they became classed as J94s; and production continued until 1963, when the last all-new pair, Nos 3880 and 3890, were built – three years after British Railways built its final steam locomotive, 9F 2-10-0 No 92220 *Evening Star*. The Hunslet pair are now both at the Buckinghamshire Railway Centre.

Hunslet is also considered to have built the final locomotive of the British steam era, in Leeds in 1971, when Kerr Stuart Brazil class type 0-4-0ST No 3902, built to a design which dated back to 1909, was supplied to the Trangkil sugar mill in Java,

the Indonesian island to which the firm made its first export a century before.

The Jack Lane works was closed in 1995, the last order being a batch of narrow gauge diesels for tunnelling on London Underground's Jubilee Line extension.

The Hunslet Engine Company, however, did not die with the rest. It passed through a succession of owners, and since its purchase from the Telfos Group in 2004, is part of the LH Group Holdings, a major specialist engineering business based at Graycar, near Burton-upon-Trent. It now owns the rights to use a lengthy list of

names, including Barclay, Greenwood & Bagtley, Hudswell Clarke and Fowler, as well as the previously mentioned firms.

LH Group Holdings chairman Graham Lee bought both Andrew Barclay and the Hunslet Engine Company as successful going concerns, not just for their historic names. He retired from the day to day running of the LH Group business in 2004, but has since been devoted to taking the Hunslet Engine company back in time.

For it is now building classic steam locomotives for sale once again, at purpose-built engineering workshops at Graham's home, Statfold Barn Farm, located just outside Tamworth in Staffordshire, where an extensive railway system complete with station, sheds, workshops and a museum has been developed on a green field site.

Although not open to the general public, occasional enthusiast open weekends are held. Those who have visited know only too well that it is a narrow gauge Mecca.

Statfold Barn Farm is also a working farm and the home of Statfold Seed Oils, a specialist natural oil company which is a major processor and supplier of natural and refined seed oils, such as flax, hemp and borage, for use in a wide range of nutritional and personal care products. State-of-the-art technology, much of it developed in-house, is used to extract, refine and bottle the oils.

The Statfold Barn Railway began as a simple oval of 2ft gauge track around the lake in the garden of Graham and his wife Carol's farmhouse.

He built a traditional engine shed from scratch and added a signalbox, complete with Great Northern Railway signalling equipment. Passenger services were provided by a Simplex diesel Charley hauling a single coach, but Graham really wanted a steam locomotive – and had problems in finding a suitable once for sale in Britain and looked much further afield.

In 2004, following extensive negotiations, he repatriated a locomotive of immense historical significance from Java – that final steam engine built by Hunslet in 1971, *Trangkil No 4*. Bought from the sugar mill it served, it was restored to as-new condition in the Statford Barn workshops. ➤

A 'real' freight carrying a harvested seed crop on the Statfold Barn Railway hauled by a Ruston four-wheeled diesel. SBR

Cabless Quarry Hunslet *Jack Lane* on the dual gauge/standard gauge flat crossing. ROBIN JONES

Orenstein & Koppel 0-4-4-0T No 1473 of 1905 *Pakis Baru No 5* is the only Mallet operating in Britain, apart from on miniature lines. The type, compact but powerful locomotives able to negotiate relatively tight curves, is named after Anatole Mallet, the engineer credited with successfully applying compounding (using steam more than once) in locomotive design. ROBIN JONES

Graham Lee driving his Hunslet Land Rover. SBR

This Baguley-Drewery diesel railcar was supplied to the French School of Military Engineering in 1919, and bought by Graham Lee from a French car dealer in 2006. Repatriated, it has been restored to original condition.
JEFF HOGAN/HUNSLET

While in Java, he visited sugar mills and was enchanted by the huge selection of early 20th century European-built steam locomotives still in existence, some working on a daily basis, others stored but steamable and some badly decayed. With the threat of imminent scrapping hanging over many, Graham was determined to rescue as many as he could.

From Pakis Baru mill, two 2ft 6in gauge Orenstein & Koppel locomotives were bought in the form of No 1, a diminutive 0-4-0 tank engine, and No 5, a substantial 0-4-4-0 compound Mallet articulated tank locomotive – a type which had never run in Britain.

At Pakis Baru, Graham caused anxiety to his Indonesian hosts by leaping into an inspection pit to examine the Mallet without first checking for any snakes, spiders and scorpions.

From Sragi mill, he bought O&K 0-6-0 tank No 14 and Krauss 0-4-2 tank No 1.

Before he could bring them back to Britain, he had to satisfy an Indonesian Government regulation banning the export of scrap metal. The engines had to be steamed first to prove that they were leaving as working locomotives.

Two more Mallets, both built by the German firm of Jung, were subsequently bought from other sugar mills.

It was obvious that Graham's garden lake railway would be far too small for most of his new acquisitions to run on, and so he developed a new running line in a field alongside.

Developed on a green field site, it offers Britain's only dual-gauge railway, combining 2ft and 2ft 6in gauge lines. There is also a short triple-gauge section, also involving standard gauge, leading to a turntable.

Furthermore, as well as searching the globe for old steam locomotives, shouldn't Hunslet be building new ones?

That is exactly what is happening in the Statfold Barn railway workshops. In 2005, the next Hunslet steam locomotive in sequence after *Trangkil No 4* appeared, in the form of No 3903. It was a classic Quarry Hunslet, just like the ones that worked in the Snowdonian slate mines, but brand new, and yours for £130,000 straight out of the box. It spent much time running on the restored section of the legendary Lynton & Barnstaple Railway at Woody Bay and toured other heritage lines as well.

They were followed by a cabless Quarry Hunslet, No 3904 *Jack Lane*, two Kerr Stuart Wren class 0-4-0 saddle tanks.

Graham now looks after the heritage and preservation connections arising from the Hunslet Engine Company's business. The 'Hunslet Steam' name has been introduced to enable enthusiasts and museums around the world to distinguish the heritage aspects of Hunslet from the firm's modern commercial operations.

The engineering works are privately owned by Graham. As well as building new ones, here he and his staff are engaged in restoring heritage locomotives and rolling stock for use both on the railway and for external customers.

He is committed to restoring all the locomotives and rolling stock in the collection to working condition for future generations to enjoy.

The journey on the dual gauge railway starts from Statfold station, the line's terminus, which was built during winter 2006/7, with two-coach trains to be operated on open days. The platform canopies include stanchions originally from South Beach station at Great Yarmouth,

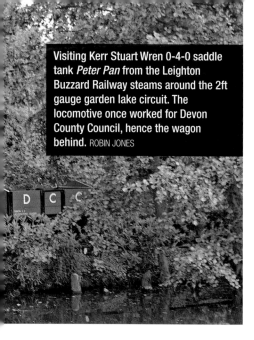

Visiting Kerr Stuart Wren 0-4-0 saddle tank *Peter Pan* from the Leighton Buzzard Railway steams around the 2ft gauge garden lake circuit. The locomotive once worked for Devon County Council, hence the wagon behind. ROBIN JONES

where they were erected by the Eastern and Midland Railway, the predecessor of the Midland & Great Northern Joint Railway.

After leaving the station, the short standard gauge line is crossed on the level, as with the Welsh Highland Railway/Network Rail crossing at Porthmadog, although the Statfold crossing has three gauges!

There is a 2ft gauge only connection with the garden lake railway.

The line then enters the Field Railway, which becomes a working industrial railway at harvest time, when seeds are collected from the combine harvester in purpose-built bulk hopper wagons. *Trangkil No 4*, which was regauged to 2ft when restored, sees regular use on the harvest at Statfold, although it is now oil seed rather than sugar cane as was the case in Java.

Oak Tree Halt has a passing loop and a platform, as well as a spur providing access to the new carriage storage shed built in 2007. From here the line continues downhill, following the perimeter of the field, to a balloon loop which enables the whole train to turn for the return journey without having to stop for the locomotive to run around.

As the Field Railway is dual gauge, a fixed crossing is provided part way around the loop to switch the 2ft gauge track from the inner and centre rails to the centre and outer rails.

The railway has become home to many less orthodox items of motive power, such as a Land Rover converted to run on rails and fitted with US-style cowcatchers, an 1880s-style bomb-shaped four-wheel locomotive which runs on compressed air and a railcar of a type which saw service in World War One.

It seems that if it runs on rails, it will be offered a home at Statfold – and it also seems that every time they hold an open weekend, there is always something either different… or very different!

• If you are interested in buying a new Hunslet steam locomotive, contact the firm on 07836 747017.

Above: *Howard,* the new Wren 0-4-0 saddle tank, works number 3905 of 2008, at Statfold. HENRY NOON

Right: Quarry Hunslet chimneys batch produced in the new Hunslet locomotive works at Statfold. ROBIN JONES

Below: The unique triple-gauge turntable at Statford station. ROBIN JONES

Pakis Baru 2ft 6in gauge Orenstein & Koppel 0-4-0 tank engine No 1 on a Statfold freight. SBR

Steam tram *Swift* hauls a passenger train around the North Ings Farm Museum line in September 2009. This is Lincolnshire's last farm railway, and was built after the others had ceased operation. ROBIN JONES

Adventures in potato land

About two decades ago, I browsed a railway bookstall and chanced upon a volume which gave me a completely new insight into the subject: Stewart E Squires' *The Lincolnshire Potato Railways* published by Oakwood Press. Never had I seen such a collection of weird and wonderful home-made railway lines, locomotives and rolling stock, private industrial systems not serving coal mines, iron furnaces, factories or docks, but potato fields, tomato greenhouses and even pigsties. I was hooked – and so was everyone who I shared the book with. Here is the unique story of a county which made a type of railway its own.

Lincolnshire is the second biggest county in England, and despite its very rural character, much of the landscape is man-made. Around a third comprises fenland reclaimed from the freshwater marshes and the sea, and turned into rich arable land.

The process did not happen overnight: in some regions, it took many centuries, and many areas which we now take for granted as dry land were still under water in Victorian times.

It was as simple a task as merely building a dyke to keep the water out: once dried out, the peat soil cracked and shrunk, lowering the land below sea level again. I know of several tarmacademed fenland road which regularly turn into roller-coaster rides when the soil on which they are laid contracts.

Once the fens were drained, however, it paved the way for agriculture. Houses were needed so that farmers could be near their livestock and crops, and new roads and cartways had to be built to bring labourers in and take produce out. Complex drainage systems and pumps were developed to keep the land dry, but in the winter months, the terrain often reverted to a quagmire.

Horse and early motor transport had its limitations here, especially in wet winters, and there were resulting problems with taking potatoes, a crop for which the reclaimed soil is particularly suitable, to market.

As Lincolnshire became enmeshed with a web of standard gauge lines, the growing of potatoes became a more lucrative crop, as there was a ready means by which they could be exported to the rest of Britain

from the major despatch centres of Boston and Spalding. Yet how do you harvest bulk crops and carry them across muddy fields so they can be taken on by train, if a main line was near enough, or by lorry to a transhipment point?

There was a simple answer: build a light railway!

In Edwardian times, potato farmer George Caudwell of St Lambert's Hall, Weston, near Spalding, inquired about building a standard gauge line on his land for the conveyance of crops. A German firm which had built lines for West Indian sugar plantations convinced him to give a 2ft gauge railway a try instead, and it was a huge success. Other farms followed his example before World War One, when similar temporary railways proved their

A car-like paraffin-fuelled steam engine pulling a wagon load of potato sacks from the Dennis Estates system at Deeping St Nicholas lines up alongside a full-size steam engine at the main line transhipment siding. STEWART E SQUIRES COLLECTION/OAKWOOD PRESS

In 1950 the Nocton potato chitting house was used for growing tomatoes, with the railway running through the centre. W REDSHAW COLLECTION/OAKWOOD PRESS

great worth on the Western Front, for which internal combustion engines were developed so as not to give the game away to the enemy with a steam locomotive emitting huge clouds of smoke.

After the war ended, a huge amount of surplus locomotives, rolling stock and track became available on the second-hand market, and more Lincolnshire farmers eagerly snapped it up to create their own railway systems.

By the late 1920s, there were at least 34 private farm railway systems in the county, with around 110 route miles – enough to build a railway from the county to London.

Few of them had locomotives: it was far easier, cheaper, more convenient and 'greener' to revert to the time-honoured method of horse traction. In some case, World War One Simplex petrol locomotives had a basic hut built over them to offer the driver some protection from the elements.

Many of the lines were concentrated around particular areas such as Deeping St Nicholas in the south, but they could be found all over the county.

The biggest system of all was the Nocton Estate Light Railway, which may have been the longest agricultural line in Britain, its 1ft 11 ½in gauge system extending to over 30 miles at its height. Having built an earlier light railway on land at Deeping St Nicholas, W Dennis & Sons began laying a similar line at Nocton in the area between Sleaford and Bardney. It was operated by army surplus light railway equipment, several Simplex diesels and briefly two steam engines.

While its main purpose was to serve potato fields, it also ascended higher ground off the fens, crossing public roads at six places, and bridged the Lincoln to Sleaford main line. The sprawling system needed its own permanent staff of drivers, guards and platelayers.

Because of crop rotation, the system also took other crops to market, including sugar beet and grain. It also played a major role in the pastoral side of the business: lines ran through pigsties from which muck was taken by wagon to be spread on the fields, through the tomato greenhouses and ➤

Motor-Rail Simplex four-wheel diesel No 1935 of 1920 *Nocton* was the first locomotive to run on the Nocton Estates Light Railway in 1920, and also the last in 1969. It afterwards became part of the Lincolnshire Coast Light Railway fleet. ROBIN JONES

Loading potatoes from the three-quarter-mile light railway at JT White's farm in Horsepit Lane, Pinchbeck, onto a solid-tyred Thorneycroft lorry in the 1920s. The railway ran to the Boston-Spalding main line, which has long since been closed and lifted. NICHOLAS WATTS COLLECTION

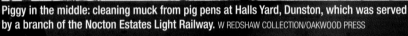
Piggy in the middle: cleaning muck from pig pens at Halls Yard, Dunston, which was served by a branch of the Nocton Estates Light Railway. W REDSHAW COLLECTION/OAKWOOD PRESS

into the mill where feed for the cattle and sheep was prepared.

At the railhead, there was a transhipment siding where produce could be loaded into standard gauge wagons in a siding off the main line at Nocton & Dunston station. Nearby was the workshop where the railway stock was maintained.

The estate railway also carried coal to the Nocton Pumping Engine, which drained most of the fen, and water not only to the cattle but to farms and cottages outside the village which had no piped supply.

Staff were regularly carried on the railway, women potato pickers who had arrived by main line train riding in empty trucks in the morning and making the return journey sitting on sacks of potatoes.

In 1927, a bogie van was converted into

Paul is another former Nocton Estates Light Railway diesel now preserved at Skegness.
ROBIN JONES

the line's only passenger coach, with sliding doors and six windows on each side, comfortable seats and a gun rack for the use of shooting parties.

The railway also carried people on Sunday school outings to the River Witham in the 1920s, and even once accommodated a funeral cortege.

The estate's main customer was Smith's Potato Crisps, which bought the land in 1936, and continued to use the railway.

After World War Two, more tractors and lorries were introduced, and while the railway was still busy, in 1955 it was decided to cut out double handling by opting for road transport altogether. Much of the railway system therefore closed by 1960, but one branch with a locomotive and four bogie wagons serving the potato chitting house soldiered on until 1969.

By then, all of the country's potato railways had gone for similar reasons. By 1945, only 17 systems and around 60 miles remained in operation. A decade later, that figure had fallen to 25 miles on three systems, including Nocton.

Yet as one door closed, another opened.

The British railway revival movement began with the saving of the Talyllyn Railway in mid-Wales by volunteers from the West Midlands in 1950, and it was followed four years later by a similar movement to restore passenger services to the moribund Ffestiniog Railway.

These were existing railways, but fresh ground was broken in 1958 when enthusiasts from Lincolnshire saved items from the Nocton Estates Light Railway and used them to build a new passenger-

carrying line on a green field site, preserving the stock and unique atmosphere of the potato railways.

The land for the railway on the edge of Cleethorpes was leased from Grimsby Rural District Council and the line opened on 25 August 1960 using a Motor Rail Simplex locomotive and a single open bogie carriage to offer genuine public transport taking holidaymakers and their heavy luggage from a bus terminus to the Humberston Fitties holiday camp and on to the beach.

In 1961, a second Motor Rail locomotive was added and the railway's first steam locomotive, Peckett 0-4-0 saddle tank No 1008 of 1903 *Jurassic*, arrived. By 1964, the line was carrying 60,000 passengers a year, and two years later it rebuilt on a new alignment. The line saw considerable

The second-time-around Lincolnshire Coast Light Railway skirted the airfield at Skegness Water Park. The Simplex locomotive is typical of those used on the Nocton Estates Light Railway, although not with the heritage era plywood body, while the coach is one of two from the 2ft gauge Ashover Light Railway in Derbyshire. ROBIN JONES

success in the late 1960s, but increasingly it struggled against competition from buses and changing holiday patterns, as more families went on cheap sunshine-guaranteed Mediterranean packages.

Much of Humberston's holiday trade came from families from the industrial north of England, and in the hardship in the wake of the miners' strike of 1984-85, passenger numbers dwindled to the point where the railway's officials could not afford to renew their lease on the trackbed.

Meanwhile, the council insisted on the installation of 6ft high fences on both sides of the railway. In 1985, faced with a series of obstacles, the railway closed and the track was lifted shortly afterwards.

However, much of the stock of the railway stayed together and a new line was built 25 miles away at the Skegness Water Leisure Park. A new passenger-carrying Lincolnshire Coast Light Railway with a somewhat unusual route along the boundary of the Skegness Aero Club's airfield publicly opened there on 3 May

2009, to widespread acclaim; with its now historically priceless Nocton stock including the line's only carriage preserved in a splendid stock and engine shed.

Anyone seriously interested in narrow gauge should visit the Lincolnshire Coast Light Railway, if only for the wealth of its museum stock, including a restored World War One ambulance van.

However, there is still one genuine farm railway running in the county.

In 1971, a 2ft gauge system was installed at North Ings Farm at Dorrington, north of Sleaford, to serve the chicken farm, handling feed, eggs and waste from cleaning of the sheds.

Although the poultry business closed in 1981, the original locomotive and wagons are still used around the farm, and have been joined by six other industrial diesel locomotives, and a freelance vertical-boilered steam tram engine named *Swift*, which began life in a different form at a traction engine club in Hockley Heath, Solihull, in 1970.

All but one of the chicken sheds have gone, but the line has been extended over the years and now forms a circuit of a third of a mile.

A passenger train provides visitors with a trip on the railway, now the centrepiece of a local private agricultural museum open on the first Sunday of the month during the summer, and includes a coach with facilities for the disabled.

Rolling stock consists mainly of industrial skip wagons, though many have been converted for other purposes, such as flat wagons, ballast and rail carriers. ∎

The only coach built for the Nocton Estates Light Railway is now preserved at Skegness. ROBIN JONES

A loading dock of the 2ft 2in gauge two-mile-long system at Vine House Farm, Deeping St Nicholas, complete with two of the four flat wagons, survives today. The horse-worked line was last used in World War Two. ROBIN JONES

Bristol's subterranean masterpiece

Sipping an ice-cool drink from the patio of the Avon Gorge Hotel in Bristol, you can enjoy one of the trademark panoramas of Britain: Isambard Kingdom Brunel's Clifton Suspension Bridge, which was completed by his admirers in 1864, five years after his death. However, in terms of Victorian engineering magnificence, the lofty bridge above the tidal Avon estuary is only one half of the story of Victorian engineering magnificence at the point of the limestone gorge; the other lies beneath the surface next to the hotel: the Clifton Rocks Railway.

Funicular or cliff railways may be considered an extreme manifestation of the 'traditional' railway concept: however, they are no means in themselves scarce.

At one stage, Britain boasted at least 35 of them, most of them built in Victorian times to serve the flourishing seaside resorts that sprang up with the growth of the railway network.

The world's oldest funicular predates the steam locomotive by three centuries. It is the Reisszug, a private line providing goods access to Hohensalzburg Castle at Salzburg in Austria and first mentioned in records dating back to 1515. Originally using wooden rails and a hemp haulage rope, it was operated by human or animal power. It is still operational today, but

employs steel rails, steel cables and an electric motor on the same route through the castle's fortifications.

Canals used inclined planes to tackle steep hills in a relatively short space of time. The Bude Canal in Cornwall, for instance, employed several of them.

Rope-worked inclines were a common feature of industrial railways; the sole surviving one in preservation today is at the Bowes Railway in County Durham.

A development of the rope-worked incline was the water-balance incline, where a wheeled water tank would be coupled to descending wagons on one of a pair of tracks, while a rope connected via a pulley would raise empty wagons on the other line. When the water carrier reached the bottom, it would be emptied, and the

empty water carrier on the train that had reached the summit refilled.

This principle was used on many funicular railways, where a water tank would be built beneath a passenger carriage.

The first funicular railway in Britain was a water-balance line opened at Scarborough in 1875, linking the town's clifftop esplanade to the spa buildings in South Bay below. Eventually, the resort had five funiculars.

What made the Clifton Rocks Railway different to the rest was that it was built underground, and had no less than four tracks (Folkestone is underground too, but only has two tracks). What's more, it served the public – and its country – well for several years after the last trains ran, and its history truly is unique.

The removal of the four cars in 1941.
FRIENDS OF THE CRR

BBC broadcasters at work in the tunnel radio station during World War Two. BBC/PATRICK HANDSCOMBE

The cable winding gear and the uppermost tracks of the railway as seen from the top station in September 2009, with a mock-up of a car front. ROBIN JONES

One of the four cars on the Clifton Rocks Railway, from a hand-coloured postcard. FRIENDS OF THE CRR

The line linked the genteel housing estates of Clifton – the 'cliff town' – with downmarket Hotwells alongside the river.

Building a cliff railway to take visitors to the beach seems a worthwhile business venture. Yet why would anyone want to link two then villages – and disparate ones too – to the west of Bristol?

Hotwells takes its name from the hot springs which bubble up through the rocks of the Avon Gorge underneath the bridge and which were first documented in 1480. In Georgian times, when spa towns were the forerunners of the Victorian seaside resorts, attempts were made to develop Hotwells as a competitor with Bath, but it never took off to anywhere near the same extent, and the waters were later found to be polluted. Hotwells fell into decline, and by the mid to late 18th century, its population included many often-drunken sailors while the Avon had degenerated into an open sewer. Clifton was only too glad it was separated from the pair by the cliffs; its population was so determined to remain apart that it even resisted the introduction of trams from Bristol city centre.

There were, however, those who were determined that Clifton should not remain in isolation. George White, founder of the Bristol Tramway Company and later the Bristol Aeroplane Company, in 1880 proposed a cliff railway from the northern end of the suspension bridge down the rockface to Hotwells, where passengers could change for the city tramway and the Bristol Port & Pier Railway and access the Hotwells landing stage from which P & A Campbell ran its pleasure steamers to Ilfracombe and South Wales. The plan stumbled against opposition from the cliffs' owner, the Society of Merchant Venturers, whose members thought it would be an eyesore.

A second scheme was similarly turned down in 1889, but the following year, publisher George Newnes, later MP for Newmarket, Cambridgeshire, submitted plans for an inclined lift from Hotwells Road to the garden of No 14 Princes Buildings, which now includes the Avon Gorge Hotel. His scheme differed from its predecessors in that it would not disfigure the cliff faces but run behind and below them in a tunnel. ➤

An early postcard of the Clifton Rocks Railway in action.

The bottom station at Hotwells, with a tram running alongside the River Avon and the suspension bridge in the background. PETER DAVEY COLLECTION

Newnes had a holiday home at Lynton in north Devon and was mainly responsible for financing the water-powered Lynton & Lynmouth Cliff Railway, designed by George Croydon Marks, later Baron Marks of Woolwich, and which opened on Easter Monday 1890, and has been running ever since. The success of the Lynton funicular began a long association between Mark and Newnes, who was also heavily involved with the building of the Lynton & Barnstaple Railway.

The Merchant Venturers agreed to this third scheme on condition that Newnes, the

Cliff railway pioneer and publishing magnate Sir George Newnes, who died at his Lynton home in June 1910, having suffered from diabetes.

sole financier, resurrected Clifton as a spa town by building a hydropathic institute next to the upper station. The Royal Clifton Spa, which had replaced Hotwells House as the main spa building in 1822, had been demolished in 1867. Newnes was happy at the compromise and appointed Philip Monroe & Sons of Baldwin Street, Bristol, as architects and CA Hayes of Thomas Street, Bristol, as contractors.

The works began on 7 March 1891 when Lady Wathen, wife of Lord Mayor Sir Charles Wathen, fired the first shot to start the tunnel excavation.

It took longer than anticipated to build, due to faults in the limestone strata which meant that the tunnel had to be lined with bricks, tripling the estimated original £10,000. The lower terminus was on Hotwells Road, close to the Bristol Port & Pier Railway's Hotwells station, and the upper in Sion Hill.

Because high traffic figures were expected for the railway, four tracks were laid with the gaslit tunnel built no less than 27ft wide and 17ft high to accommodate them.

Each line was 450ft long over a 1-in-2.1 gradient and built to 3ft 2in gauge, and there was a fleet of four 18-seater cars, each with its own brakeman. The cars were operated as connected pairs using the water-balance method. The water emptied from the cars into a reservoir at the lower station was pumped back to one at the upper one by four-stroke gas engines. A cabin at the upper station housed the railway controller who was equipped with a handbrake for the cable pulley sheaves.

The railway was officially opened on 11 March 1893 when 6220 passengers made the return trip. The fares were a penny to go up and four pence to go back down, the journey taking 40 seconds. On that first day, each passenger received a commemorative gilded white metal

medallion in the shape of a Maltese cross with a representation of one of the cars on one side together with the initials of the promoter, engineer and architect. The first year saw 427,492 passengers carried, including 110,000 in the first six weeks: however, this proved to be the all-time high, and afterwards numbers steadily dropped.

In 1894 the Clifton Spa Pump Room, designed by Philip Munro, was opened next to the upper terminus as promised. It drew spa water from Hotwells via a 350ft borehole. Four years later, it was joined by the Clifton Grand Spa Hydro which had landscaped gardens extending down to the river.

On 29 September 1912 the railway was bought by the Bristol Tramways & Carriage Co Ltd, operator of the city's electric tramways, for £1500 after it had gone bankrupt.

In a bid to boost patronage of the funicular line, the company introduced a threepenny ticket for a round trip from the city centre to Hotwells by tram, up the cliff railway and back into Bristol by bus.

However, a major blow to the Clifton Rocks Railway came in 1922 when the Bristol Port & Pier Railway closed.

As with railways elsewhere, serious competition was presented by the new and more versatile bus services – which finally killed off the cliff railway. It last operated on 29 September 1934 and its demise was followed five years later by that of the city's tram system, which also could not compete with buses.

However, a new chapter in the story of the Clifton Rocks Railway began in 1940, when, along with the former Pump Room, by then converted to a cinema, was taken over by Imperial Airways (later to become British Overseas Airways) who built an office suite and used part of the upper section of the tunnel for storage and repair of barrage balloons.